Technology Strategy Essentials: A Concise Guide and Primer
© 2023 by Bharat Rao

Notice of Rights

Liability Disclaimer

TECHNOLOGY STRATEGY ESSENTIALS

A Concise Guide and Primer

BHARAT RAO

 MINDZEN MEDIA

TECHNOLOGY STRATEGY ESSENTIALS

A Concise Guide and Primer

The goal of this book is to provide a clear and concise overview of key frameworks and models that are essential for developing effective technology strategy, making it an ideal resource for students, entrepreneurs, and managers.

Written in a brisk and easy-to-read format, the book covers a wide range of topics, including the technology life cycle, innovation diffusion, disruptive innovation, open innovation, intellectual property, and first-mover advantage, among many others. Each topic is presented in a condensed but structured manner with real-world case examples that illustrate key concepts and strategies. An indispensable guide for individuals seeking to gain a comprehensive understanding of the core concepts of technology strategy, along with their practical application is now within your reach.

Bharat Rao is a researcher, educator, and author. He is Research Professor in the Department of Technology Management and Innovation Management at New York University's Tandon School of Engineering. He is also the author of *Marketing Essentials: A Concise Guide and Primer, Magical: How Magic and its Star Performers Transformed the Entertainment Economy,* and *Defense Technological Innovation: Issues and Challenges in an Era of Converging Technologies.*

Foreword

I have been teaching graduate and undergraduate students, as well as managers and executives, about technology strategy, marketing, and global innovation for more than two decades, both at New York University and other universities and forums. Some of the students from my first classes are now seasoned executives, founders, and venture capitalists. Over the years, I have seen how the field of technology strategy has evolved, both from research and applied standpoints. In my classes, I have focused on teaching the many interesting ideas that make up this field. I've also used a lot of real-world examples and case studies that students can solve together in class.

So that I could keep track of the information I learned over the course of a semester, I have kept detailed notes on both well-known and emerging themes in technology strategy. My goal was to create concise notes that I could hand out to students as supplementary readings at the end of each class, both to review at their leisure (or for exams) and as a resource to refresh their knowledge anytime they wished, even after graduation. The book you hold in your hand is a compilation of all these notes, but put together in a more organized form. I have used GPT4 as a research and writing assistant to organize my notes over the years to add some structure and flow while keeping the content direct, focused, and engaging. All content, data sources, and case examples have been checked for accuracy and relevance.

I envision that this book will be used as a simple guide and primer. You do not have to start at Page 1 and proceed linearly through the rest of the book. You can freely jump to any chapter or section and expect to get a quick summary of the topic in question. You can also return to a topic you would like to brush up on, or consider some alternate ideas and resources to solve your problem. Happy reading!

TECHNOLOGY STRATEGY ESSENTIALS

A Concise Guide and Primer

TABLE OF CONTENTS

CHAPTER I

Technological Change and Innovation

Why Technology Strategy?

We are undoubtedly living in an era of accelerated innovation. New products, services, and industries have come about because of how quickly technology and related domains are changing and getting better. From the rise of smartphones and social media to the emergence of self-driving cars and renewable energy, innovation has transformed the way we live, work, and interact with each other. The COVID-19 pandemic has sped up innovation even more as businesses and people have gotten used to the new normal of remote and hybrid work, telemedicine, and online commerce. Also, governments and organizations all over the world are putting a lot of money into research and development to find solutions to global problems like climate change, healthcare, and cybersecurity. With the growth of new technologies like AI, blockchain, and quantum computing, we can expect innovation to be a constant change agent and catalyst for many years to come.

Many experts now believe that we are on the road to approaching the 'singularity' in the not-to-distant future. The singularity is a concept that was popularized by futurist and inventor Ray Kurzweil, and refers to a hypothetical point in the future (possibly 2045) when the convergence of multiple cutting-edge technologies, including artificial intelligence, surpasses human intelligence and capabilities, leading to an exponential increase in technological progress and changes in society and the economy that are difficult for us to predict or control. Some experts believe that we will see AGI within the next decade if not earlier, especially after considering the early successes of several LLMs (large language models), including OpenAI's ChatGPT, Microsoft's Bard, Claude from Anthropic, Google's Gemini, and many others.

Taking a step back and looking at the present, it is obvious that in order to fully participate in and harness the power of innovation in the current economy, we require systematic conceptual understanding, as well as analytical tools and frameworks to analyze ongoing developments and translate our analysis into action. The discipline of technology strategy is applicable in this situation. As you can guess, the term "strategy" refers to a high-level plan or approach to achieving a certain goal or target. Often, a strategy takes a long-term perspective and seeks to develop a sustainable competitive advantage.

Technology strategy is simply a logical way to plan how to use technology to assist a company in achieving its goals and objectives. It entails identifying and selecting the technologies that best meet the requirements of the business while also ensuring that they are consistent with the overall business plan. Technology management and optimal utilization are also included in technology strategy in order to enhance performance, obtain a competitive edge, and add value for customers and stakeholders. A technology plan may also include solutions to problems with cybersecurity, data management, and other technological concerns that are crucial to an organization's success.

It is critical to remember that business investments in technology R&D must be consistent with the overall strategy of the organization. Although the concept is simple, the implementation is not always straightforward. According to research by Chris Pappas published in the Journal of Product Innovation Management, the process of developing a firm's strategy typically prioritizes financial factors and market share over technology. To put the company on the path to long-term competitive advantage, technology strategy must be prioritized and thoughtfully integrated into corporate planning. Technology innovation has long been proven to boost competitive performance, productivity, and profitability. So there is a compelling case to be made for putting technology strategy first and allowing it to guide overall corporate strategy and vision.

Research and development, innovation, product development, intellectual property, technology acquisition and licensing, strategic alliances and partnerships, technology commercialization, and technology governance are just a few of the many subjects that fall under the umbrella of technology strategy. Across a wide range of industries, including information technology, telecommunications, biotechnology, pharmaceuticals, energy, manufacturing, consumer goods, and many more, the principles and frameworks of technology strategy can be applied. Recent advancements in fields like artificial intelligence, blockchain, genomics, and omics have further expanded the domains to which many of the fundamental principles of technology strategy are applicable. These new technologies have the power to disrupt existing sectors and generate entirely new ones, which might give rise to brand-new business models and methods of wealth creation. As a result, firms must carefully consider their technology strategy if they want to remain competitive and relevant in today's rapidly evolving business climate. Likewise, the fundamental concepts of technology strategy are drawn from a variety of disciplines, such as science, engineering, management strategy, economics, and public policy, to name a few.

Defining Innovation

When we talk about innovation, we are referring to the *process of creating something new* or *improving upon an existing product, process, or service*. It involves a spectrum of activities, from identifying a problem or an opportunity to developing a novel solution that has value in the marketplace. Innovation can take many forms, including technological breakthroughs, new business models, creative marketing strategies, and social innovations that address complex social problems. Innovation is critical for economic growth, job creation, and competitiveness, as it allows businesses and individuals to differentiate themselves in the marketplace and stay ahead of the competition.

At this point, it is useful to review some important definitions of innovation and the people or organizations associated with them:

> *Innovation is the "specific tool of entrepreneurs, the means by which they exploit change as an opportunity for a different business or a different service."*
> *– Peter Drucker*

4

Innovation is "the introduction of something new, a new idea, method or device." – **Merriam-Webster Dictionary**

"Companies achieve competitive advantage through acts of innovation. They approach innovation in its broadest sense, including both new technologies and new ways of doing things." – **Michael Porter**

Innovation is "the creation, development and implementation of a new product, process or service, with the aim of improving efficiency, effectiveness or competitive advantage." – **The European Commission**

Innovation is "the implementation of a new or significantly improved product (good or service), or process, a new marketing method, or a new organizational method in business practices, workplace organization or external relations." – **The Oslo Manual**

Innovation is "the successful exploitation of new ideas" *–* **The UK Department of Trade and Industry**

Innovation is "the design, invention, development, and/or implementation of new or altered products, services, processes, systems, organizational structures, or business models for the purpose of creating new value for customers and financial returns for the firm."
– **The Conference Board**

Innovation is "the process of creating, developing and diffusing new ideas, goods and services, and improving

> *organizational and institutional arrangements for*
> *implementing them in the marketplace and in society."*
> – The OECD (Organization for Economic Cooperation and
> Development)

Taken together, these definitions show how important creativity, novelty, and creating value are in the process of innovation, as well as the potential benefits for both the organization doing the innovating and its customers or society as a whole.

Managing Technological Change

A related term we encounter in technology strategy is that of 'managing technological change'. Others refer to this as MTI or 'managing technological innovation'. These terms are part of the bigger process of managing how an organization introduces and uses new technologies. It involves figuring out how new technologies might affect an organization's operations, processes, and products and figuring out what changes need to be made to make the switch to the new technology go smoothly.

The purpose of managing technological change is to reduce the disruptions and issues that frequently accompany the introduction of new technologies while maximizing the benefits and possibilities that they provide. This necessitates meticulous preparation, communication, and collaboration throughout the company. Managers can direct the organization toward the ultimate aim of sustainable competitive advantage by properly implementing these techniques.

Effective management of technological change involves several key steps, including:

1. **Assessing the impact of the technology:** This involves evaluating the potential impact of the technology on the organization's operations, processes, products, and stakeholders.

2. **Developing a plan:** Based on the assessment, a plan should be developed that outlines the necessary steps and resources required to successfully implement the technology.

3. **Communicating the plan:** Effective communication is essential to ensuring that all stakeholders are aware of the plan and their roles in its implementation.

4. **Training and support:** Adequate training and support should be provided to employees to ensure they have the skills and knowledge needed to work with the new technology.

5. **Monitoring and evaluation:** Once the technology has been implemented, it is important to monitor its performance and evaluate its impact on the organization.

In today's fast-paced and highly competitive business climate, "managing" technological change is critical. Despite changing external conditions in the technological environment, adoption of such a stance enables firms to remain innovative and competitive while also assuring the efficiency and effectiveness of their operations and processes. Organizations may reap the benefits of new technologies while minimizing the challenges by properly managing technological change.

Formulating Strategy: Mintzberg's View

The management scholar Henry Mintzberg has proposed several key ideas that help us deal with technological change and innovation. In particular, his views challenge the traditional approach rooted in strategic planning, and suggest that strategy can be dynamic and evolve in response to new challenges. We can summarize some of Mintzberg's key ideas as follows:

1. Strategies can be both deliberate (planned and intended) and emergent (arising from patterns of action that were not initially intended).

2. Strategy can be viewed through five different perspectives, or "Ps": Plan, Ploy, Pattern, Position, and Perspective. By considering these various aspects, managers can better understand and formulate their organization's strategy.

3. It is important that there be a continuous, iterative process for strategy development. Rather than relying solely on formal planning processes, organizations should be more adaptive and responsive to their environment, thus allowing for the emergence of new strategies.

4. An organization's structure plays an influential role in its ability to effectively develop and implement strategic initiatives.

Overall, Mintzberg's work on strategy focuses on how strategic management is always changing, how important it is to look at things from different points of view, and how organizations need to be able to change and adapt to their surroundings. This works especially well in the field of technology, which is always changing and moving.

What are the Sources of Innovation?

Innovation can come from a variety of sources, including internal and external ones. By leveraging these sources, organizations can create new products and services that meet customer needs and stay ahead of industry trends.

Here are some of the key sources of innovation:

1. **Customers:** Many successful products have been developed based on customer feedback and insights. For example, Apple's iPod was created in response to the need for a portable music player that could store large amounts of music in a compact device. The design and features of the iPod were based on feedback from customers, who wanted a device that was easy to use and had a long battery life. Note that the functionality of the iPod was later subsumed by the iPhone, and the iPod itself was discontinued by Apple.

2. **Employees:** Employee input can also lead to innovative products and services. Google's "20% time" policy, which allows employees to spend 20% of their work time on personal projects, has led to the development of many new products, including Google News and Gmail. Of course, there are numerous examples of former employees of well-known companies starting ventures on their own, either to pursue new

opportunities, or because their previous employers did not recognize or support their initiatives.

3. **Partners and suppliers:** Collaborating with partners and suppliers can also lead to innovation. Nike, for example, developed its innovative "Flywire" technology in collaboration with its suppliers. Flywire is a lightweight and durable material used in the construction of athletic shoes that has improved the performance and comfort of Nike's products. It has allowed Nike to engineer shoes that are both lightweight and responsive.

4. **Competitors:** Keeping an eye on competitors can also lead to innovation. For example, Uber was developed in response to the need for a more convenient and efficient transportation option than traditional taxis. By identifying the shortcomings of the existing taxi industry, Uber was able to create a new and innovative service that disrupted the market.

5. **Research and development:** Investing in research and development can lead to the creation of new technologies and products. Tesla, for example, has invested heavily in the research and development of electric vehicle technology, which has enabled it to create innovative products like the Model S and Model X. Tesla's R&D investments have allowed it to take the lead in powertrain technologies, long-range batteries, supercharger network infrastructure, and other critical areas.

6. **Emerging technologies:** Exploring emerging technologies can also lead to innovation. For example, Microsoft's HoloLens is a

mixed-reality headset that enables users to interact with virtual objects in the real world. This innovative technology has a lot of possible uses, from games and entertainment to making things and teaching. Investing in long-range research and development can yield technological breakthroughs that redefine industries. The product has been adopted by leading organizations, including NASA and the US Army.

Innovating through "Lead Users"

The idea of "lead-user innovation" is a big source of new ideas that has been growing in recent years. "Lead user innovation," as the name suggests, is the technique of involving imaginative and forward-thinking customers in the development of new products or services. Lead users are people who possess a high level of knowledge, zeal, and drive in a certain field and who are more likely to have needs and issues that current solutions have not yet been able to resolve. They usually do better than the market as a whole when it comes to identifying trends, needs, and solutions. One characteristic that distinguishes lead users is that some of them, after correctly identifying the issue, attempt to develop a solution on their own. Their lack of excitement about practicing their idea is their biggest problem. This could be due to a lack of information or resources to commercialize their ideas, or, in some cases, a lack of financial resources, market expertise, or production capabilities required to bring a product to market. These lead users used to be happy to use their own answers and go on to the next problem, but today such inventors have the option of collaborating with other parties that are interested in commercialization. Advanced lead users might be more willing to take the initiative by sharing their ideas with businesses that can benefit from them than the other way around. Lead user innovation strives to collect these innovations and integrate them into the creation process.

The development of new surgical instruments, a field that has been fertile ground for many new creative innovations, is a good example of lead user innovation. Surgeons frequently deal with unique practical problems that necessitate cutting-edge equipment. They might create brand-new tools to address these problems, but they frequently lack the funding, know-how, or enthusiasm to promote these tools widely. If they are successful in overcoming these obstacles, these surgeon-inventors might be able to license their inventions to businesses that produce and market medical devices. For instance, vascular surgeon Dr. Tom Fogarty created the Fog Light.

Lead User Innovation Process

Firms can use lead user innovation to develop new products by identifying lead users, involving them in the development process, and leveraging their knowledge and expertise to create solutions that meet the needs of a broader customer base. The following are some simple steps that a firm can take to use user innovation to develop new products:

1. **Identify lead users:** The first step is to identify lead users in the target market. This can be done through market research, social media, online forums, and other channels.

2. **Involve lead users:** The next step is to involve the lead users in the development process. This can be done through various

methods, such as focus groups, online communities, co-creation workshops, and other participatory techniques.

3. **Leverage lead user knowledge:** The firm should leverage the knowledge and expertise of the lead users to develop new products. This can be done by using their insights to identify unmet needs, develop concepts, and test prototypes.

4. **Refine and test prototypes:** The next step is to refine and test prototypes based on the feedback received from lead users. This will help to ensure that the new product meets the needs of a broader customer base.

5. **Launch and market the product:** Once the product is refined, the firm can launch and market it to a broader customer base.

Examples of lead user innovation include:

- Lego's Mindstorms, a robotic construction set that was developed with the help of lead users who were interested in building robots with Lego blocks.

- 3M's Post-it Notes, which were developed based on feedback from lead users who wanted a way to temporarily attach notes to paper.

- Volkswagen's Golf GTI is a sports car that was developed with the help of lead users who wanted a car that was both practical and sporty.

The following steps make up a straightforward plan that a company can use to use lead user innovation while creating a new product:

1. Identify a target market and the needs of the customers.

2. Identify potential lead users who have a high level of expertise, interest, and motivation in the target market.

3. Engage with the lead users to understand their needs and problems, and to generate ideas for new products.

4. Develop prototypes of the new product, based on the insights and feedback from the lead users.

5. Test and refine the prototypes, based on the feedback from the lead users.

6. Launch the new product and market it to a broader customer base.

Research has shown that lead-user innovation can lead to significant benefits for companies, including improved product performance, reduced development costs, a faster time to market, and increased customer satisfaction. One study published in the Journal of Product Innovation Management found that companies that used lead user innovation had higher success rates in new product development and achieved greater sales growth and profitability than those that did not use this approach. Another study published in Research Policy found that lead user innovation can result in higher-quality products and lower development costs compared to traditional R&D approaches. This approach to creating new products is gaining traction in several industries, given these advantages.

Rapid Prototyping and Rapid Experimentation

Lead user innovation is often closely linked to rapid prototyping and rapid experimentation, which are both ways to test and develop new product ideas quickly and effectively. Working with innovative customers, or "lead users," to create new products or services that meet their unique and changing needs is called "lead user innovation." Rapid prototyping and experimentation, on the other hand, involve making and testing prototypes of new products or services quickly and efficiently. This method lets companies try out and improve their ideas before investing a lot of money and time in mass production. Rapid prototyping and experimentation can help companies identify design flaws, reduce development costs, and speed up time to market. Thus, these practices can go hand-in-hand, as they complement each other very well. By combining lead user innovation with rapid prototyping and experimentation, companies can make products or services that are not only new but also meet the needs of their target customers. This approach can help companies gain a competitive advantage in the market by delivering products or services that are tailored to the unique needs of their customers.

Professor Eric von Hippel of MIT, who first introduced the concept of lead user innovation, has also conducted research on the role of rapid prototyping in the innovation process. In his book "Democratizing Innovation," von Hippel talks about how important it is to use rapid prototyping to test and improve product ideas quickly and cheaply, especially when lead users are part of the design process. Similarly, Stefan Thomke, a professor at Harvard Business School, has studied the use of rapid experimentation in the innovation process, and has argued that rapid experimentation is key to achieving success in product development. He emphasizes the importance of quickly testing and iterating on product ideas in order to identify and address potential problems early on in the process. These can lead to reduced costs and time to innovate, improved innovation quality, an increased success rate, and enhanced organizational learning. Developing a facility for rapid experimentation can thus be a critical competitive edge in industries with dynamic changes in underlying technologies and market conditions.

CHAPTER II

Technological Standards

The concepts of technology standards and dominant design play a critical role in the success of any technology. Standards make sure that different products can work together and with each other, and dominant designs create a set of features and characteristics that define a technology. In this chapter, we'll talk about how important these things are for innovation and technology strategy. We will look at how standards and dominant designs start, change, and affect how new technologies are used and spread. We will also talk about the difficulties of setting and managing standards, as well as the benefits and risks of dominant designs.

What are Standards?

Technological standards are sets of rules, specifications, or guidelines that define how products or services should work, communicate, or be designed. To guarantee the interoperability, compatibility, dependability, and safety of technology products and services, numerous organizations—including industry consortiums, international standards bodies, and government agencies—develop and maintain them.

Technological standards have changed over time because technology has gotten better, more people want things to work together, and business is becoming more global. In the early days of technology, individual businesses or industry associations frequently developed standards to establish proprietary systems or defend their market positions. Over time, however, standards have become more formalized, open, and inclusive, as more stakeholders have been involved in their development and implementation.

Some examples of important technological standards that impact our lives every day include:

1. **Internet Protocol (IP):** a standard protocol for transmitting data over the internet, developed by the Internet Engineering Task Force (IETF).

2. **IEEE 802.11 (Wi-Fi):** a set of standards for wireless local area networks (WLANs), developed by the Institute of Electrical and Electronics Engineers (IEEE).

3. **USB (Universal Serial Bus):** a standard interface for connecting computer peripherals, developed by the USB Implementers Forum (USB-IF).

4. **ISO 9001:** a set of quality management standards for organizations, developed by the International Organization for Standardization (ISO).

5. **HTML (Hypertext Markup Language):** a standard language for creating web pages, developed by the World Wide Web Consortium (W3C).

6. **Bluetooth:** a standard for wireless communication between devices, developed by the Bluetooth Special Interest Group (SIG).

7. **MPEG (Moving Picture Experts Group):** a set of standards for digital audio and video compression, developed by the International Organization for Standardization (ISO) and the International Electrotechnical Commission (IEC).

Technological standards play a critical role in shaping the development and adoption of technology, enabling innovation, and ensuring interoperability and compatibility across different products and services. Without these standards, we would find chaos and disorder, instead of a predictable and systematic way of getting things done using technology.

Why Do Standards Matter?

Standards play an essential role in promoting technological innovation for several reasons:

1. **Interoperability:** Standards help to ensure that different products and systems work together seamlessly. This promotes compatibility and interoperability, enabling users to integrate products and services from different vendors and promoting competition and innovation. Standards can help to avoid vendor

lock-in, where users are restricted to a single vendor's products and services because of proprietary interfaces or protocols.

2. **Quality:** Standards can help to ensure that products and services meet certain quality and safety requirements. This can be particularly important for products that involve public safety or health, such as medical devices or transportation systems. Standards can also provide guidelines for best practices, leading to better quality products and services.

3. **Cost Reduction:** Standards can help to reduce costs by promoting economies of scale and reducing duplication of efforts. When different products or systems use the same standards, it becomes easier and more cost-effective to design, manufacture, and maintain them. This can make technology more accessible and affordable for a wider range of users, promoting adoption and innovation.

4. **Innovation:** Standards can promote innovation by providing a common language and framework for technology development and use. By defining standards, different stakeholders can come together to collaborate on new technologies and share knowledge and expertise. Standards can also create a level playing field for competition, which can spur innovation and drive new developments.

We can safely argue that standards are crucial to technological innovation as they provide a foundation for interoperability, quality, cost reduction, and innovation. By enabling different products and systems to work together seamlessly and promoting quality and safety requirements, standards help to make technology more accessible, affordable, and innovative for all.

Dominant Designs

A dominant design is a specific configuration or set of features that becomes widely accepted as the industry standard for a particular product or service. It is a commonly adopted solution to a problem that becomes accepted as the norm in the market. There are a number of factors that affect the emergence of a dominant design, such as:

1. **Technological breakthroughs:** The introduction of a new technology that can serve as a platform for future innovation can accelerate the emergence of a dominant design.

2. **Market competition:** Intense competition in the market can lead to a convergence of features and a homogenization of products, eventually leading to the emergence of a dominant design.

3. **Customer preferences:** Customer demand and preferences can influence the development of a dominant design. Over time, customers may come to prefer a particular feature set or configuration, leading to the adoption of a dominant design.

4. **Standards development:** The establishment of technical or industry standards can contribute to the emergence of a dominant design by providing a common language and framework for the development and adoption of products and services.

5. **Learning and network effects:** As more users adopt a particular design, this can lead to network effects that further reinforce the dominance of that design. Users become more familiar with the design and more willing to invest in products and services that conform to it, further solidifying its position as the dominant design.

Overall, the emergence of a dominant design reflects a dynamic interplay between technological, market, and social factors and can have significant implications for the development and adoption of technology products and services.

How Dominant Designs Emerge

Prior to the emergence of a dominant design, there is a period of tumult or incremental innovation in which multiple alternatives are developed and compete for market share. Firms use this time to conduct research and development in order to improve their products and gain a competitive advantage. As firms test new ideas and approaches, the market is characterized by a high degree of uncertainty and experimentation.

Firms create a diverse set of product alternatives as they experiment with new ideas. Some of these alternatives prove more successful than others over time, and they begin to gain market share. As the market evolves, a few successful alternatives emerge and begin to dominate it. This is known as selection.

The familiar phenomenon of imitation takes control when a small number of options start to rule the market. Businesses start copying popular products and modifying them to fit their particular needs. A dominant design, or widely adopted product architecture or technology, is the end result of this process and becomes the norm for the industry.

During the incremental innovation phase, there is a lot of experimentation and uncertainty, and businesses need to be flexible and sensitive to market developments. They must continually assess their products and tactics if they are to stay competitive and react to new trends. Once a dominant design has emerged, businesses must concentrate on enhancing and perfecting their products within that framework in order to keep their competitive edge.

The Case of QWERTY

Many English-language keyboards still employ the QWERTY keyboard layout. In order to stop the keys on mechanical typewriters from jamming, Christopher Sholes, the inventor, first devised QWERTY in the 1870s. The arrangement places frequently used letter pairings on opposite sides of the keyboard, forcing the typist to switch between using both hands. By doing this, the possibility of neighboring keys being pressed simultaneously and jamming the mechanism is decreased.

Even though the QWERTY layout was ostensibly made to prevent jamming, it is often called inefficient and ugly because it requires a lot of finger movement and can slow down typing speeds. However, QWERTY became the dominant keyboard layout for a number of reasons:

1. **Early adoption:** When Sholes introduced the first typewriters, he also began selling them to businesses and government agencies.

These early adopters became accustomed to the QWERTY layout and continued to use it, even as newer and more efficient keyboard layouts were developed.

2. **Network effects:** As more people learned to type on QWERTY keyboards, the layout became the standard in the industry. This made it more difficult for new keyboard layouts to gain traction, as users were already familiar with QWERTY and preferred to stick with what they knew.

3. **Cost and infrastructure:** As more typewriters were produced with QWERTY layouts, it became more expensive to switch to a different layout. This was especially true for businesses and government agencies, which had invested heavily in typewriters and training for their employees.

4. **Patents and intellectual property:** Sholes held a number of patents related to typewriters and the QWERTY layout, which made it difficult for competitors to develop and market alternative layouts.

QWERTY emerged as a dominant design for mechanical typewriters due to a combination of early adoption, network effects, cost and infrastructure, and patents and intellectual property. Despite being inefficient and inelegant, it has remained in use due to its familiarity and the difficulty of transitioning to a different layout. Today, it is still used on many English language keyboards, although there are now many alternative layouts available that offer more efficient typing. The case of

QWERTY clearly demonstrates the importance and long-term impacts of dominant designs.

'Creative Destruction' and the links to Innovation

Joseph Schumpeter (1883-1950) was a renowned Austrian economist and one of the most influential thinkers in the field of innovation. He is known for his work on the theory of economic development, in which he argued that innovation is the driving force behind economic growth and prosperity.

Schumpeter's main contribution to the field of innovation was the concept of "creative destruction." He argued that the process of innovation involves the destruction of old industries and the creation of new ones. This process is necessary for economic growth and leads to the creation of new products, services, and markets. Creative destruction is thus the process by which new technologies, products, and business models replace old ones. It involves the creation of new markets, products, and services that displace existing ones. The market's competitive forces, which encourage businesses to develop new and improved products in order to stay one step ahead of their rivals, are what propel this process.

Here are some examples of industries shaped or reinvented by creative destruction:

1. **The music industry:** The rise of digital music and distribution and the decline of physical media like CDs and vinyl records is a classic example of creative destruction. The introduction of new technologies like MP3 players and online music streaming

services disrupted the traditional music industry, leading to the decline of record stores and the rise of new digital platforms.

2. **The retail industry:** The rise of e-commerce and online shopping has disrupted the traditional retail industry. Brick-and-mortar stores are facing increasing competition from online retailers like Amazon, which offer lower prices and greater convenience.

3. **The transportation industry:** The rise of ride-sharing services like Uber and Lyft has disrupted the traditional taxi industry. These services offer lower prices, greater convenience, and improved safety, leading to the decline of traditional taxi services in many cities.

4. **The telecommunications industry:** The rise of smartphones and mobile internet has disrupted the traditional telecommunications industry. These new technologies have enabled consumers to access the internet and communicate with each other in new and innovative ways, leading to the decline of traditional landline telephone services.

At the end of the day, creative destruction is a crucial step in the invention process. By continuously creating new goods and services and getting rid of outdated ones, the market is able to adjust to shifting customer demands and tastes, leading to increasing economic growth and wealth. We find that some firms perform better than others at foreseeing and bringing about change, despite the idea that creative destruction will virtually likely modify the corporate environment.

Numerous research have been done to find out why some businesses succeed and grow over time.

The lifespan of a firm is influenced by a complex set of factors, including its industry, competitive environment, and internal management practices. Some firms thrive for only a few years, while others survive for multiple decades and even centuries. Sustained success in the marketplace requires a combination of factors that enable a firm to adapt to changing market conditions, maintain a competitive advantage, and meet the needs and expectations of its customers. Several factors can contribute to sustained success in the marketplace:

1. **Innovation:** Innovation is a critical factor in long-term success. Firms that are able to develop and introduce new products and services that meet the changing needs and preferences of their customers are more likely to thrive over the long term.

2. **Adaptability:** Firms that are able to adapt to changing market conditions are more likely to succeed over the long term. This requires a willingness to embrace change, invest in new technologies and processes, and develop new business models to meet evolving customer needs.

3. **Customer focus:** Successful firms have a deep understanding of their customers' needs and preferences. They use this knowledge to develop products and services that meet these needs and build long-term relationships with their customers.

4. **Strong leadership:** Effective leadership is critical to sustained success. Strong leaders are able to develop and communicate a

clear vision for the firm, build and motivate a talented team, and make strategic decisions that position the firm for long-term success.

5. **Financial management:** Sound financial management is essential for long-term success. Firms that are able to generate consistent revenue and profitability, manage costs effectively, and maintain a strong balance sheet are better able to weather economic downturns and invest in future growth.

6. **Culture:** A strong culture that values collaboration, creativity, and innovation can help firms sustain success over the long term. A culture that encourages open communication, continuous learning, and risk-taking can foster the development of new ideas and initiatives that drive innovation and growth. In addition, the firm needs to be attuned to the broader social culture and era it is operating in, and understand the changing needs and wants of its customers.

The Types of Innovation

Architectural innovation refers to a type of innovation that changes the way the various components of a product or system are interconnected while maintaining the core design concepts. In other words, architectural innovation reconfigures the relationship between existing components without changing the components themselves. Abernathy and Clark, two leading scholars in technology management, used this notion to provide a framework for understanding innovation (in 1985). Their framework is based on an understanding of two these underlying dimensions along which innovation can be classified, i.e. component change and architectural change. They are described as follows:

1. **Component Change:** This dimension focuses on the degree to which an innovation alters the core components or elements of a product, system, or technology. A high component change means that the innovation involves significant modifications or replacements of the existing components, whereas a low component change indicates that the core components remain mostly unchanged.

2. **Architectural Change:** This dimension concerns the degree to which an innovation changes the relationships, interactions, or interconnections among the components of a product, system, or technology. A high architectural change implies that the overall structure, organization, or configuration of the system is significantly altered, while a low architectural change means that the existing architecture is mostly maintained.

Based on these two underlying dimensions, innovations can now be classified into four categories based on the degree of change they introduced to the existing components and the architecture of a system. These categories are:

1. **Incremental innovations:** Minor improvements or changes to existing components and architecture.

2. **Modular innovations:** Significant changes to one or more components, while the overall architecture remains the same.

3. **Architectural innovations:** Changes in the relationships among components or the way they are interconnected, without altering the core components themselves.

4. **Radical innovations:** Fundamental changes to both the components and the architecture of a system, leading to the creation of entirely new products or systems.

The table below illustrates how these types of innovations differ, both in terms of the underlying dimensions of component change (COMP) and architectural change (ARCH), along with suitable examples:

Category	COMP Change	ARCH Change	Description	Examples
Incremental	Low	Low	Minor improvements or changes to existing components and architecture.	Software updates, improved battery life, fuel efficiency
Modular	High	Low	Significant changes to one or more components, with the overall architecture remaining the same.	New camera sensor in a smartphone, improved engine in a car
Architectural	Low	High	Changes in relationships among components or their interconnections, without altering the components.	Transition from mainframe to personal computers
Radical	High	High	Fundamental changes to both components and architecture, creating entirely new products or systems.	Film to digital photography, development of the Internet, electric vehicles

Table: The Types of Innovation

Disruptive Innovation

A term popularized by the Harvard Business School professor Clayton Christensen, 'disruptive innovation' describes the process through which new products or services gain a foothold in the market and eventually displace established competitors. This phenomenon has led to significant changes in various industries, affecting the competitiveness and survival of incumbent firms. Christensen's work on disruptive innovation began with the publication of his seminal book, "The Innovator's Dilemma: When New Technology Cause Great Companies to Fail."

Periods of normal and periods of disruption define innovation by determining the level of competition, the pace of change, and the potential for new market entry. During periods of normal innovation, established firms focus on incremental improvements to existing products, leading to a predictable rate of change and a stable competitive environment. In contrast, during periods of disruptive innovation, new entrants and startups gain footholds in the market by providing innovative solutions to unmet needs, leading to rapid and unpredictable changes in the competitive landscape. This often results in a decline of established firms that fail to adapt to the new environment, while new and innovative firms rise to prominence.

Christensen argues that companies must be aware of and prepared for disruptive innovation in order to remain competitive and sustain success over the long term. He describes a disruptive innovation as one that starts in a niche market and eventually replaces an existing technology or process by providing a simpler, cheaper, or more convenient solution.

Here is a summary of the key factors that contribute to the success of disruptive innovations:

1. Incumbents often focus on high-profit segments and sustaining innovations, neglecting the potential threats posed by disruptive innovations.

2. Disruptive innovations often start as inferior products or services, targeting lower-end or unserved markets. This allows them to gain a foothold without directly competing with incumbents.

3. As disruptive innovations improve, they can move upmarket, eventually capturing a larger share of the market and displacing incumbent firms.

The impact of disruptive innovation on firms and industries has been profound. Some popular examples include:

1. Digital photography displaced film photography, with companies like Kodak facing significant challenges as a result.

2. The rise of e-commerce platforms like Amazon, which disrupted traditional brick-and-mortar retail stores.

3. The advent of streaming services like Netflix, which revolutionized the entertainment industry and led to the decline of DVD rental stores and traditional cable TV.

4. The rise of ride-sharing services like Uber and Lyft, have disrupted the traditional taxi industry by offering a more

convenient and affordable alternative. The ease of use and flexibility of ride-sharing apps allowed them to quickly gain popularity among consumers. Additionally, the ability to rate drivers and receive real-time updates on the status of their ride improved the overall customer experience. As the popularity of ride-sharing grew, traditional taxi companies struggled to compete, and many were forced out of business. Today, ride-sharing services are an integral part of the transportation industry and have transformed the way people travel.

We can also see a similar phenomenon in the case of 3D printing, as described in more detail below:

Case Example: 3D Printing

3D printing, also known as additive manufacturing, has experienced significant growth and development since its inception in the 1980s. The technology has the potential to disrupt traditional manufacturing methods and revolutionize various industries, including aerospace, automotive, and healthcare. Let us take a look in brief at the historical evolution of 3D printing, its expanding capabilities, and examples of its applications in different industries.

The history of 3D printing can be traced back to the early 1980s when Charles Hull invented stereolithography. This initial development laid the foundation for subsequent advances in additive manufacturing technologies, such as Fused Deposition Modeling (FDM) by S. Scott Crump in the late 1980s and Selective Laser Sintering (SLS) by Dr. Carl Deckard in the early 1990s. The growth of 3D printing technologies accelerated in the 21st century, driven by improvements in materials, software, and hardware, as well as the expiration of key patents that led to increased competition and innovation.

Recent advances in 3D printing have expanded its potential uses and capabilities. For example, the technology can now process a wide range of materials, including metals, ceramics, and even living cells for bioprinting applications. Advancements in software and hardware have also made 3D printing more accessible and user-friendly, allowing individuals and small businesses to leverage its benefits. Furthermore, innovations in areas such as multi-material printing and in-situ material recycling have opened up new possibilities for product design and manufacturing.

Some examples of industrial applications of 3D printing include:

1. **Aerospace:** 3D printing has made significant inroads in the aerospace industry, with companies such as GE Aviation and Airbus using the technology to create complex, lightweight components that reduce material waste and improve fuel efficiency. The technology has also been used to produce satellite components and rocket engines, demonstrating its potential for high-precision, high-value applications.

2. **Automotive:** The automotive industry has embraced 3D printing for the production of prototype parts, custom components, and tooling. Companies like BMW and Ford have integrated 3D printing into their design and manufacturing processes, allowing for faster development cycles and greater design freedom.

3. **Healthcare:** In the healthcare sector, 3D printing has been employed to create patient-specific implants, prosthetics, and medical devices, as well as anatomical models for surgical planning and training. Additionally, research into bioprinting has the potential to revolutionize regenerative medicine by enabling the creation of living tissue and organs for transplantation.

3D printing has clearly evolved significantly since its inception, and continues to disrupt traditional manufacturing methods. Its expanding capabilities and applications across various industries demonstrate its potential to fundamentally change the way products are designed, manufactured, and distributed. By enabling the creation of complex, customized products at a low cost, 3D printing has the potential to reduce barriers to entry for new competitors and reshape the global manufacturing landscape.

Case Example: Generative AI

Generative artificial intelligence (AI) is a fast developing technology that has the potential to transform the way we work and interact with machines. Generative AI refers to AI systems that can generate fresh content that is indistinguishable from human-created output, such as text, photos, and videos. Over the next few decades, this highly disruptive technology has the potential to drastically alter labor markets while boosting global productivity.

According to a recent Goldman Sachs analysis, generative AI might automate up to 40% of present human labor. Some industries, such as customer service and manufacturing, may face severe employment losses as a result. However, the paper expects that generative AI will generate new jobs in fields such as software development and design.

Another study conducted by Stanford University found that generative AI could benefit the economy as a whole. According to the Stanford report, generative AI has the potential to enhance productivity and generate totally new market opportunities. The study also discovered that generative AI could aid in the resolution of some of the world's most urgent grand challenge problems, such as climate change and poverty.

Overall, generative artificial intelligence has the capacity to both disrupt and generate jobs. It is critical to carefully analyze the potential impact of generative AI on the workforce and to design policies that will help ensure that this new technology benefits everyone. While substantial ambiguity surrounds its capacity and adoption timeframe at the present time, recent discoveries indicate that AI is well-positioned to expand swiftly and scale in the years ahead.

CHAPTER III

New Product Development (NPD)

Developing a new product (or service) is one of the most essential but also challenging and resource-intensive processes that can determine the success or failure of a company. This chapter provides an overview of the new product development (NPD) process and the challenges involved in bringing a new product to market. We discover the critical stages of the NPD process, including idea generation, concept development, product design, testing and validation, commercialization, and deployment. Additionally, the chapter addresses the typical resources and time requirements necessary for successful NPD, as well as strategies for managing these resources effectively.

A company that successfully masters the new product development (NPD) process is well-positioned for long-term success because it is a difficult skill to develop that is required for growth and innovation. Among its advantages are the possibility of gaining a sustainable competitive advantage, increased revenues, and increased profitability. However, the challenges of NPD should not be underestimated, and businesses must be willing to invest the necessary resources and expertise to succeed.

What is NPD?

New product development (NPD) is the process of bringing a new product to market. It is an important aspect of marketing and involves a series of steps, from idea generation to commercialization, that help companies bring new and innovative products to their customers.

Typical Stages in the NPD Process

The NPD process typically involves several stages, including:

1. **Idea generation:** This is the starting point of NPD, where companies gather ideas for new products from various sources. One method to generate new ideas is to encourage brainstorming sessions where team members can openly share their thoughts and ideas without any judgment. This can be done through techniques such as mind mapping or word association exercises. Another way is to gather insights from customers through surveys, focus groups, or interviews. By understanding their needs and pain points, companies can develop new solutions that meet their customers' needs. Additionally, companies can foster a culture of experimentation by encouraging employees to take risks and try out new ideas, even if they fail. Hackathons, crowdsourcing and innovation challenges can also be effective ways to generate new ideas by bringing together individuals from different departments or even different companies to collaborate on solving a specific

problem. NASA, for example,has been using hackathons and crowdsourcing to generate new ideas and spur innovation. Hackathons are events where participants gather to collaborate and develop new solutions to a specific problem or challenge. NASA has organized several hackathons in recent years, inviting participants to create solutions for challenges ranging from space exploration to environmental sustainability.

2. **Concept development:** In this stage, companies evaluate the viability of different ideas and choose the best ones to pursue. The evaluation phase of concept development involves assessing each idea's potential by considering factors such as market demand, technological feasibility, and financial feasibility. Companies need to evaluate each idea's potential to determine whether it aligns with their strategic goals and objectives and whether it has the potential to provide a sustainable competitive advantage. Once the evaluation is complete, companies typically choose the most promising ideas to move forward to the concept development stage. This stage involves developing a detailed concept of the product, including its features, benefits, and target market. The company needs to understand its customers' needs and preferences and how the product will fit into their lives. Companies may conduct market research, gather feedback from potential customers, and conduct focus groups to gather information about their target market. They also develop a detailed concept of the product, including its features, benefits, and target market.

3. **Market research:** Market research is a critical stage in the new product development process. Companies need to understand the market landscape to identify the target audience, their preferences, and willingness to pay for the product. Market research can help companies identify gaps in the market and identify potential competitors. By understanding the competitive landscape, companies can develop strategies to differentiate their products and gain a competitive advantage. Market research also helps companies evaluate the potential demand for the product and estimate its potential revenue. Market research methods can vary depending on the product and target audience. Methods can include surveys, focus groups, and online research. Surveys can be used to gather data on customer preferences, purchase behavior, and demographics. Focus groups can provide more detailed insights into customer attitudes, opinions, and behaviors. Online research can provide insights into customer behavior and trends. By conducting market research, companies can make informed decisions about the viability of their product and identify potential barriers to success.

4. **Product design and development:** Product design and development is a crucial stage in the new product development process that requires careful planning, execution, and monitoring. During this stage, companies work to transform their concepts and ideas into tangible products that meet customer needs and preferences. One key aspect of this stage is the creation of prototypes, which allows companies to test and

refine their product designs before launching them on the market. This helps to identify and correct any design flaws, defects, or functionality issues early in the development process, which can save time and money in the long run. Companies also need to ensure that their products comply with all relevant regulations and standards, such as safety and environmental requirements, to avoid potential legal and reputational risks. To develop a successful product, companies need to follow a structured and iterative process that involves continuous testing, feedback, and refinement. This may involve working closely with suppliers, partners, and customers to gather insights and identify areas for improvement. Companies also need to consider factors such as product functionality, user experience, packaging, pricing, and branding during the design and development process. The goal is to create a product that offers unique features, benefits, and value propositions that differentiate it from competitors and meet the needs of the target market. Ultimately, a well-designed and developed product can help companies gain a competitive advantage and achieve long-term success in the market.

5. **Commercialization:** Commercialization is the final stage of the NPD process and marks the culmination of efforts put in by the company to bring a new product to market. This stage involves the development and implementation of a comprehensive marketing strategy aimed at introducing the new product to potential customers. The objective of commercialization is to make the product available to the target audience and drive sales.

The process of commercialization involves several activities, such as market research, advertising, pricing, and sales promotion. Companies may also use different channels, such as online sales, retail stores, and direct sales, to make the product available to customers. One of the critical factors in the success of commercialization is the marketing strategy. Companies need to develop a marketing plan that is aligned with the overall business strategy and takes into account the target market, competitive landscape, and customer preferences. Companies need to focus on creating awareness about the product, communicating its benefits to customers, and creating a sense of urgency to drive sales. The pricing strategy is also essential in commercialization, as it plays a critical role in determining the product's market position and revenue potential. Companies need to set the right price point that reflects the product's value and is competitive in the market. Successful commercialization requires effective coordination between different departments within the company, such as marketing, sales, and distribution, to ensure that the product is launched successfully and meets the company's objectives.

As can be seen from the steps above, the NPD process is essential to a company's success as it allows them to keep pace with changing market trends, consumer preferences, and technological advancements. By continuously introducing new and innovative products, companies can attract new customers, retain existing ones, and gain a competitive advantage in their industry. Moreover, the NPD process enables companies to differentiate themselves from their competitors and create a unique value proposition for their customers.

The NPD process also helps companies optimize their resources and investments by reducing the risk of failure. By conducting market research, prototyping, and testing, companies can identify potential issues and weaknesses in their products before launching them to the market. This reduces the likelihood of expensive failures and enables companies to make informed decisions about which ideas to pursue and which to abandon. Furthermore, by utilizing a structured NPD process, companies can improve their overall efficiency, reduce the time to market, and maximize the return on investment.

Challenges in NPD

New product development (NPD) can be a complex and challenging process, and there are several challenges that companies may face along the way. Some of the most common challenges include:

1. **Resource constraints:** Developing a new product can be resource-intensive, requiring significant investments of time, money, and manpower. Companies may face challenges in obtaining the necessary resources to bring a new product to market.

2. **Uncertainty:** There is always some level of uncertainty involved in NPD, as it can be difficult to predict how customers will respond to a new product. Companies may also face unexpected challenges during the development process, such as changes in regulations or technological advancements.

3. **Competition:** The market is often highly competitive, and companies may face challenges from established players and new entrants. Companies must be aware of their competitors' products and strategies and be prepared to respond to new challenges.

4. **Timing:** Launching a new product at the right time is crucial for success. If a company launches a product too soon, it may not be ready for the market, while if it launches too late, it may miss out on opportunities.

5. **Customer preferences:** Companies must be attuned to customer preferences and needs, as these can change rapidly. Companies must be able to adapt to changing customer preferences and respond to new trends in the market.

6. **Market acceptance:** There is always a chance that a new product won't be well-received by the public. Companies must be prepared for the possibility of low sales or a lack of customer interest and be prepared to modify their product or marketing strategy accordingly.

Despite these challenges, the rewards of successful NPD can be significant, and many companies have been able to overcome these challenges to bring innovative and successful products to market. By staying attuned to customer needs and the market and making informed decisions throughout the NPD process, companies can increase their chances of success.

NPD Differences Across Industries

The process of new product development (NPD) can vary significantly across industries in terms of practicality, cost, and effectiveness. Some of the factors that can impact NPD in different industries include:

1. **Industry complexity: The** complexity of the industry can impact the NPD process in terms of the amount of research and development required, the complexity of the product design, and the regulatory requirements. For example, industries such as pharmaceuticals and aerospace require much more research and development, and are subject to more stringent regulations, than industries such as consumer goods or fashion.

2. **Product life cycle:** The life cycle of a product can impact the cost and practicality of NPD. For example, in industries with short product life cycles, such as fashion or technology, companies must be able to bring new products to market quickly and at a lower cost in order to stay competitive.

3. **Competition:** The level of competition in an industry can impact the cost and effectiveness of NPD. In highly competitive industries, companies may have to invest more in research and development, marketing, and distribution in order to bring new products to market.

4. **Customer preferences:** The preferences of customers in different industries can also impact the NPD process. For example, in industries where customers are highly price-sensitive, such as

groceries or consumer electronics, companies may need to focus on developing low-cost products in order to be successful.

5. **Technology:** The state of technology in an industry can also impact NPD. For example, in industries where technology is rapidly advancing, such as biotechnology or renewable energy, companies may need to invest in research and development in order to stay ahead of the competition.

These are just a few of the factors that can impact NPD across different industries. The specific challenges and opportunities of NPD in any given industry will depend on the unique combination of these and other factors.

The Costs of NPD

The cost of new product development (NPD) can vary significantly depending on the type of product being developed. Here are three simple illustrative examples that discuss the cost of NPD for a few different types of products:

1. **New car:** Developing a new car can be a highly complex and expensive process, requiring significant investments in research and development, testing, and manufacturing. The cost of NPD for a new car can range from several hundred million dollars to over a billion dollars, depending on the size and scope of the project.

2. **New drug:** Developing a new drug can be an even more complex and expensive process than developing a new car. The cost of

NPD for a new drug can range from hundreds of millions of dollars to over a billion dollars, depending on the complexity of the research and development process and the regulatory requirements. See the case example on the pharmaceutical industry before.

3. **New soap:** Developing a new soap is typically a less complex and less expensive process than developing a new car or a new drug. The cost of NPD for a new soap may range from tens of thousands of dollars to several million dollars, depending on the scope of the project and the marketing and distribution costs.

It's important to note that these are rough estimates, and the actual cost of NPD for any given product will depend on many factors, such as the size of the company, the scope of the project, and the competition in the market. Additionally, the cost of NPD can vary significantly even within a single industry, as different companies may have different levels of resources and expertise, and may adopt different strategies for bringing new products to market.

Case Example: Auto Industry

The development of a new car involves several stages and expert teams. To begin, the design team creates a concept for the car's shape and then uses CAD programs or clay models to bring it to life. Mechanical engineers then work on the metal, plastics, and glass, while powertrain engineers work on the car's power generation and transmission. While production engineers plan how the car will be manufactured, lighting, electrical, and electronics engineers work on the car's lights and electronics. To develop the car, all of these teams collaborate with engineering teams from suppliers. Millions of dollars are spent on developing models and prototypes, as well as testing everything in wind tunnels, test tracks, public roads, and crash testing. The final cost could range between tens and hundreds of millions of dollars.

As a result of high development and production costs, large volume manufacturers like Toyota earn a profit of around $2,500 per car sold. Porsche sells cars ranging from $50,000 to $150,000, with an estimated profit of $17,000 per car. This implies that the cost of production for each car is between $33,000 and $133,000. Ford earns a gross margin of $2,200 on each car sold for around $22,000, putting the cost of production at approximately $20,000. Ferrari's high-end sports cars can cost upwards of $200,000, but the manufacturer only makes around $6,000 per car. This indicates that the cost of production could be as high as $195,000. These dynamics have also changed with the emergence of EVs. An examination of financial data has revealed that Tesla's profit per vehicle manufactured is significantly higher compared to Toyota, by a factor of eight. Despite producing fewer vehicles in Q3 2022 than Toyota, Tesla outperformed the Japanese company in terms of profitability. According to Nikkei Asia, Tesla's profit margin per vehicle in Q3 2022 was eight times greater than Toyota's, with Tesla reporting a net profit of $3.29 billion and Toyota reporting $3.15 billion in the same period.

Case Example: Pharmaceutical Industry

Perhaps no other industry exemplifies the huge amount of investment of time, capital and other resources to new product development than the pharmaceutical industry. The process of getting a drug to market typically involves several critical steps. Here is a general overview:

The process of getting a drug to market typically involves several critical steps. Here is a general overview of the steps involved in getting a pharmaceutical drug to market in the United States:

1. **Discovery and Preclinical Development:** In this stage, researchers identify a promising compound and conduct preliminary laboratory tests to assess its potential as a drug. They may also conduct animal studies to evaluate its safety and effectiveness.

2. **Clinical Development:** Once a promising compound has been identified, it undergoes several stages of clinical trials to test its safety and effectiveness in humans. These trials typically involve three phases:

    a. Phase 1: Small-scale trials in healthy volunteers to assess safety and dosage levels.

    b. Phase 2: Larger trials in patients to evaluate effectiveness and side effects.

    c. Phase 3: Large-scale trials in patients to confirm effectiveness and monitor side effects.

3. **FDA Review:** After the completion of clinical trials, the drug company submits a New Drug Application (NDA) to the U.S. Food and Drug Administration (FDA) for review. The FDA reviews the NDA to determine if the drug is safe and effective for its intended use.

4. **Approval and Commercialization:** If the FDA approves the drug, it can be marketed and sold to the public. The drug company will typically invest in marketing and distribution to ensure the drug reaches patients who need it.

Stage	Description	Time Required	Cost
Discovery and Preclinical Development	Identify a promising compound and conduct preliminary laboratory tests to assess its potential as a drug. Conduct animal studies to evaluate its safety and effectiveness.	3 to 6 years	$100 million to $500 million
Clinical Development	Conduct trials to test the drug's safety and effectiveness in humans.	6 to 7 years	$100 million to $500 million
FDA Review	Submit New Drug Application (NDA) to the FDA for review. FDA reviews the NDA to determine if the drug is safe and effective for its intended use.	2 years	$2 million to $3 million
Approval and Commercialization	If approved, the drug can be marketed and sold to the public. The drug company will typically invest in marketing and distribution to ensure the drug reaches patients who need it.	N/A	N/A

Table. Typical Stages of New Drug Development

The entire process of getting a drug to market can take several years, with some estimates suggesting it can take up to 10-15 years or more. The cost of developing a new drug can also be significant, with estimates ranging from $2.6 billion to $3 billion.

Successful pharma blockbusters include drugs like Lipitor (atorvastatin) for high cholesterol, Humira (adalimumab) for rheumatoid arthritis and other autoimmune diseases. Before the FDA approved them and marketed them to the general public, these medications all underwent extensive clinical testing. The companies that developed these drugs invested significant time and resources in the research and development process, but ultimately saw significant returns on their investment.

As per 2023 data by PhRMA, a trade group representing pharmaceutical companies in the US, it costs an average of $2.6 billion and takes 10-15 years to develop a single new medicine, which includes the cost of many failed attempts. Moreover, only 12% of new molecular entities that enter clinical trials receive approval from the U.S. Food and Drug Administration (FDA). While approximately 7,000 rare diseases exist, only 5% have available treatments. The biopharmaceutical pipeline currently has close to 260 vaccines in development to prevent and treat diseases, including dozens specifically for COVID-19. As can be seen, in such competitive and highly regulated industries, the costs of new product development are indeed astronomical. Firms need to be very careful and deliberate about the avenues they pursue when new opportunities for candidate drugs present themselves.

The table below shows costs across industries for specific products that were developed:

Industry	Company	NPD Cost ($ millions)	Product Developed
Automotive	General Motors	1000	2022 Chevrolet Silverado EV Truck
Consumer Electronics	Samsung	150	Galaxy S10 Smartphone
Pharmaceuticals	Johnson & Johnson	800	Spravato for Treatment-Resistant Depression
Software	Microsoft	1,000	Windows 11
Aerospace	Boeing	15,000	Boeing 787 Dreamliner
Consumer Goods	Procter & Gamble	750	Tide Eco-Box Detergent Packaging
Automotive	Tesla	1,500	Tesla Model S
Telecommunications	Verizon	1,000	5G Network Buildout

Table: Sample NPD Costs by Industry

Can the NPD Model be Used for Services?

The development of a new service can follow a similar pattern to the development of a new product, but there are some differences in the processes and challenges involved. In both cases, there are typically stages of idea generation, market research, prototyping, testing, and commercialization. However, the development of a service is often less tangible and more intangible than the development of a physical product, which can affect the research, testing, and commercialization stages.

In addition, the development of a new service may involve more emphasis on customer experience and co-creation with customers, as services are often highly personalized and customized to meet individual customer needs. The marketing and pricing strategies for services may also differ from those for products, as services are often sold based on the intangible value they provide rather than the physical features and benefits.

Overall, while there may be some similarities in the development of new services and new products, the unique characteristics of services require a tailored approach to NPD that takes into account the specific challenges and opportunities presented by the service sector.

CHAPTER IV

Teams and Team Dynamics in NPD

Teams and team dynamics can be critical to the success of new product development, and there are several common issues that can arise:

1. **Poor communication:** Communication breakdowns can occur when team members fail to share information effectively or misunderstand each other, which can lead to delays, rework, and errors.

2. **Lack of trust:** Without trust, team members may be reluctant to share ideas, give and receive feedback, or take risks. This can lead to missed opportunities and a lack of creativity.

3. **Role confusion:** Team members may be unclear about their roles and responsibilities, leading to confusion and duplication of effort. This can also create tension and conflict between team members.

4. **Resistance to change:** Resistance to change can be a significant barrier to innovation. Team members may be resistant to new ideas or new ways of doing things, which can stifle creativity and limit the potential of new products.

5. **Groupthink:** Groupthink can occur when team members are too focused on maintaining consensus and harmony, at the expense of critical thinking and constructive feedback. This can lead to poor decision-making and missed opportunities.

6. **Lack of diversity:** Teams that lack diversity may struggle to generate new and innovative ideas. Teams with diverse perspectives and backgrounds can bring different insights and experiences to the table, which can lead to more creative solutions.

7. **Poor leadership:** Strong leadership is essential for successful new product development. Without effective leadership, teams may lack direction, fail to prioritize tasks effectively, or struggle to stay on track.

These issues can contribute to the high failure rates of new product development projects. Addressing these issues requires a combination of effective leadership, clear communication, and a willingness to embrace change and new ideas.

Cross-Functional Teams

Cross-functional teams are made up of people who work together on a project or task but come from different backgrounds and have different kinds of skills. The team typically consists of members from different departments, such as marketing, engineering, design, and operations, among others. The goal of cross-functional teams is to get people with different skills and points of view to work together to solve hard problems and come up with new ideas. For example, when a new car model is being made, a group of people from different departments would work together to run the project. The team might have engineers who are in charge of designing the car's mechanical parts, designers who are in charge of making the car's exterior and interior look good, marketing experts who are in charge of finding out what customers want and need, and manufacturing experts who make sure the car can be made quickly and cheaply.

The size and composition of cross-functional teams can have a significant impact on project outcomes. When it comes to team size, bigger teams may have more resources and experts at their disposal, but they may also have trouble communicating and working together. Smaller teams may be faster and better at communicating, but they may not have the right skills or resources.

Aside from the size of the team, the make-up of the cross-functional team is another important thing to pay close attention to. Having a wide range of skills and points of view can help people solve problems better and come up with more creative solutions. But different backgrounds and ways of working can also make the team feel tense and cause problems. Also, team members may have different priorities or goals based on the goals of their departments, which can make it hard to get everyone working toward the same goal.

Overall, it's important for cross-functional teams to have clear goals, good communication, and a culture of working together and respecting each other so that they can get the most out of different points of view while avoiding problems.

Case Example: Boeing 787 Dreamliner

In aircraft design, cross-functional teams are essential to creating safe, efficient, and reliable aircraft. These teams typically include members from engineering, design, aerodynamics, materials science, manufacturing, and testing, among others. Each member brings unique expertise and knowledge to the project, allowing the team to tackle complex problems and create innovative solutions.

The development of the Boeing 787 Dreamliner involved a cross-functional team that included over 50 suppliers and partners from around the world. The team was responsible for designing and manufacturing various components of the aircraft, including the engines, wings, fuselage, and avionics. One of the key challenges facing the team was the development of the aircraft's composite materials. The Dreamliner was the first commercial airliner to be made primarily from composites, which offered significant weight savings and improved fuel efficiency compared to traditional aluminum alloys.

To develop these new materials, the cross-functional team had to collaborate closely with materials scientists and manufacturing experts. They had to test various composite materials and manufacturing processes to ensure that they met stringent safety and quality standards while also being cost-effective and scalable for large-scale production. The team's efforts paid off, and the Dreamliner became one of the most successful commercial aircraft in history, with over 1,400 orders from airlines around the world. The use of cross-functional teams was a critical factor in the success of the project, as it allowed the team to leverage the expertise of individuals from different backgrounds to create a truly innovative and groundbreaking aircraft.

Typical Team Structures

Since each project has unique characteristics, requirements, and goals, the type of team required may be different. These projects may also need different levels of cross-functional integration, coordination, and control. Choosing the appropriate team structure can help optimize team performance, enhance communication and collaboration, and increase the chances of project success. Some commonly used team structures are noted below:

1. Functional Teams are teams where members report to their respective functional managers, and they may spend less than 10% of their time on a specific project. Typically, there is no project manager or dedicated liaison personnel, and there is little opportunity for cross-functional integration. Functional teams are likely to be appropriate for derivative projects.

2. Lightweight Teams are similar to functional teams, but they typically have a project manager and dedicated liaison personnel. Members may spend less than 25% of their time on a project, and the project manager is usually a junior or middle manager. Lightweight teams are likely to be appropriate for derivative projects.

3. Heavyweight Teams are collocated with the project manager, who is typically a senior manager with significant authority to command resources and evaluate members. While they may still be temporary, core team members are often dedicated full-time to the project. Heavyweight teams are likely to be appropriate for platform projects.

4. Autonomous Teams are collocated and dedicated full-time (and often permanently) to the team, with the project manager being a very senior manager. The project manager is given full control over resources contributed by functional departments and has exclusive authority over the evaluation and reward of team members. Autonomous teams may have their own policies, procedures, and reward systems that differ from those of the rest of the firm. Autonomous teams are likely to be appropriate for breakthrough and major platform projects, although it can be difficult to fold them back into the organization.

Team Administration and Management

Team administration and management play a critical role in the success of a project. For heavyweight and autonomous teams, it is common practice these days to have them develop a project charter and a contract book. The project charter outlines the project's mission, goals, and key success criteria. It is a tool that serves as the guiding star for the team in case they run into conflicts or doubts. It also typically describes the team's composition, the length of time members will spend on the team, and the team budget. While this can change over the duration of the project, the idea is to have a good sense of the direction and scope of the project at the outset. The contract book, on the other hand, provides a detailed plan to achieve the goals laid out in the charter. It includes estimates of resources required, a development time schedule, and expected results. By symbolically signing the contract book, team members establish a sense of commitment and ownership over the project. This process helps to ensure that the team remains focused on achieving the project's goals, and it provides a tool for monitoring and evaluating the team's performance.

In addition to the project charter and contract book, team administration and management can also involve establishing communication and reporting protocols, defining roles and responsibilities, and developing a plan for managing risks and issues that may arise during the project. Three additional aspects to be carefully considered include:

1. **Effective communication:** This is critical for ensuring that everyone on the team is on the same page and working towards the same goals. This can include regular team meetings, status updates, and progress reports. It's important to establish clear lines of communication and identify who should be involved in each communication exchange.

2. **Defining Roles and Responsibilities:** These should be clearly defined to avoid confusion or duplication of effort. This can involve creating job descriptions or task lists for each team member and ensuring that everyone understands their specific responsibilities and the contributions they are expected to make to the project.

3. **Risk Management:** This is an important aspect of team administration and management, and one that is frequently neglected until too late. It involves identifying potential risks to the project, assessing the likelihood and impact of each risk, and developing strategies to mitigate or manage them. For example, if a key team member is unexpectedly unavailable, there should be a plan in place to redistribute their workload or bring in a replacement if necessary.

Overall, effective team administration and management are critical for ensuring that the team is working together efficiently and effectively towards a common goal. If done properly, the process can establish clear expectations, improve communication, and minimize the risk of project delays or failures. Effective team administration and management are critical to ensuring that projects are completed on time, within budget, and to the required quality standards.

Virtual Teams

Virtual teams are groups of people who work together on a specific project or task while being located in different physical locations, often in different time zones, and relying on technology to communicate and collaborate. Unlike traditional teams, virtual teams use communication technologies such as email, video conferencing, instant messaging, and online collaboration tools to work together. In recent years, several factors have accelerated the use of virtual teams, in small organizations and large. These include:

1. **Advancements in technology:** With the widespread availability of high-speed internet and collaboration tools, it is now easier

than ever to communicate and work together remotely. Video conferencing, file sharing, and project management tools have made it possible for teams to work together seamlessly, even if they are located in different parts of the world.

2. **Globalization:** As businesses continue to expand globally, it is becoming increasingly common for teams to be geographically dispersed. Virtual teams allow organizations to tap into talent from around the world, without the need for team members to relocate.

3. **Cost savings:** Virtual teams can help organizations reduce costs associated with office space and other overhead expenses. This can be particularly beneficial for small businesses and startups with limited resources.

4. **Work-life balance:** Virtual teams can offer more flexibility and allow team members to work from home, which can be beneficial for those who need to balance work with other responsibilities, such as caring for children or elderly parents.

5. **The COVID-19 pandemic:** The pandemic forced many organizations to adopt remote work arrangements to comply with social distancing measures. During this time Zoom went from being an obscure platform to a verb in the English language. The pandemic and its aftermath has led to an increased reliance on virtual teams, with many organizations now considering making remote work a permanent option. Further,

many employees are seeking jobs which offer them opportunities for virtual or hybrid work.

While virtual teams offer many benefits, they also come with a number of challenges. These include:

1. **Communication barriers:** Communication can be more challenging in virtual teams, especially when team members are located in different time zones or have limited access to reliable internet.

2. **Lack of trust:** Without the opportunity for face-to-face interaction, team members may struggle to develop trust and rapport with one another.

3. **Cultural differences:** Virtual teams may consist of members from different countries or cultures, which can lead to misunderstandings and communication challenges. Language barriers are another issue although English has become the defacto global language of business.

4. **Technology issues:** Technical problems can arise, such as poor internet connectivity or compatibility issues with software and hardware.

5. **Management challenges:** Managing a virtual team can be more challenging than managing a traditional team, as managers may struggle to monitor progress and ensure accountability.

The case examples below illustrate how virtual teams have been deployed in practice and can be used to solve critical problems and challenges. With the constant improvements in technology, as well as changing attitudes and expectations towards the nature of work itself, it is clear that virtual teams are here to stay.

Case Example: Coca-Cola Life

One early example of the use of a virtual team is the Coca-Cola Life project. In 2013, Coca-Cola set an ambitious goal to launch a new product, a reduced-calorie soda called Coca-Cola Life. To accomplish this, Coca-Cola formed a virtual team consisting of members from several countries. The team used technology such as video conferencing, instant messaging, and collaborative software tools to work together and communicate effectively despite being physically located in different parts of the world. They also established clear roles and responsibilities, established deadlines, and regularly reported on their progress to ensure that they stayed on track.

Thanks to the success of this virtual team, Coca-Cola was able to launch Coca-Cola Life in Argentina in June 2013, and eventually in the US in 2014.

Case Example: Watson Anywhere

In 2018, IBM launched a virtual team to develop a new AI-powered product called Watson Anywhere, which allows businesses to use IBM's Watson artificial intelligence technology in any cloud environment. The virtual team was made up of developers and engineers from different locations across the globe, including the United States, Canada, Germany, and India. The use of a virtual team allowed IBM to bring together the expertise and knowledge of individuals from different locations and time zones, enabling the company to develop the product faster and more efficiently. Additionally, the use of virtual collaboration tools, such as video conferencing and online project management software, facilitated communication and coordination among team members. By 2019, Watson could run on any cloud environment including competitor platforms like AWS, Azure and Google Cloud. By 2020, over 300,000 developers, data scientists and others were collaborating on Watson projects all over the globe.

The success of the virtual team was evident in the rapid development and launch of Watson Anywhere, which has since become an important product for IBM in the AI market. The use of a virtual team also allowed IBM to save on travel costs and office expenses, demonstrating the potential cost benefits of virtual teams.

Role of the Team Leader

In any team-based project, the role of team leader can make a significant difference to the outcome of the project. Team leaders are responsible for guiding the team towards achieving the goals of the project. They are in charge of managing and coordinating the team's efforts, ensuring that everyone is working towards the same objectives, and resolving any conflicts that arise.

The team leader is typically chosen based on their expertise in the subject matter of the project, their leadership skills, and their ability to work effectively with others. They may be chosen by the organization or may emerge as a leader within the team based on their skills and contributions. Their responsibilities are varied: they include setting expectations for team members, delegating tasks, monitoring progress, providing feedback and support, and ensuring that the project is completed on time and within budget. They must be able to motivate team members and keep them focused on the end goal, as well as be able to communicate effectively with stakeholders and management. The team leader thus plays a crucial role in the success of the project and must be able to adapt to changing circumstances and challenges that may arise.

When dealing with virtual teams, the team leader needs to use some special criteria to ensure project success. Firstly, the team leader needs to select team members who are self-motivated, proactive, and able to work independently, as well as have the skills and experience needed to perform their assigned tasks. The team leader should have enough knowledge and confidence in the team members abilities so that they can work remotely without much direct supervision. Secondly, the team leader needs to establish clear communication channels and protocols, as well as set expectations for responsiveness and availability. Thirdly, the team leader needs to establish processes for managing conflict and resolving disputes among team members, given that conflicts can be more difficult to resolve in a virtual environment. Finally, the team leader needs to ensure that the team has access to the necessary technological infrastructure and support to work effectively, including reliable internet connectivity and secure communication tools.

Culture Matters

Research has shown that organizational culture plays a crucial role in promoting or hindering innovation within a company. The culture of an organization reflects its values, beliefs, and norms, and these factors shape the attitudes and behaviors of its employees. A culture that supports innovation can be a key driver of growth and success, while a culture that discourages risk-taking and experimentation can stifle creativity and lead to stagnation. While it is one thing to have effective managers or teams, their overall impact will be greatly magnified if they exist in an organizational environment that encourages and supports them, and gives them the resources and knowledge to grow.

There are several strategies that companies can use to create a culture of innovation. As pointed out earlier, one of them is to encourage open communication and collaboration among employees. When employees feel comfortable sharing ideas and working together, it can lead to the creation of new products, services, and processes. This can be facilitated through team-building activities, cross-functional projects, and open-door policies.

Another strategy is to provide employees with the resources and support they need to be innovative. This can include funding for research and development, access to cutting-edge technology, and training and development programs. Companies can also establish innovation labs or centers of excellence that are dedicated to exploring new ideas and technologies.

Company	Innovation Lab Location	Key Activities
Google	Mountain View, CA	Autonomous vehicles, AI, quantum computing
Amazon	Seattle, WA	Alexa voice assistant, Amazon Go stores, drones
Microsoft	Redmond, WA	HoloLens, AI, quantum computing
IBM	Yorktown Heights, NY	Quantum computing, AI, blockchain
Samsung	Mountain View, CA	5G, AI assistant Bixby, AR/VR
Intel	Hillsboro, OR	Neuromorphic computing, quantum computing
Facebook	Menlo Park, CA	Augmented reality, AI assistants
Apple	Cupertino, CA	Machine learning, AR/VR, autonomous systems
Uber	Pittsburgh, PA	Self-driving car technology
Toyota	Palo Alto, CA	AI, robotics, autonomous driving

Table. Innovation Labs of Selected Tech Leaders

Companies can also foster a culture of innovation by recognizing and rewarding employees who demonstrate creativity and initiative. This can include offering bonuses, promotions, or other incentives for successful innovation projects. Companies can also create formal recognition programs to acknowledge employees who have made significant contributions to the company's innovation efforts. Moreover, companies can encourage employees to share their ideas and collaborate with others through brainstorming sessions or innovation workshops. By providing a supportive environment for innovation, companies can not only improve their bottom line but also attract and retain top talent.

It is important for companies to recognize that creating a culture of innovation requires a long-term commitment. This involves not only providing resources and support but also establishing a mindset that values creativity, risk-taking, and continuous improvement. Companies that are successful in creating a culture of innovation are often those that are willing to challenge the status quo and embrace change.

There are many examples of companies that have successfully created a culture of innovation. One example is Google, which is known for its "20% time" policy that allows employees to spend one day a week working on personal projects. This has led to the creation of several successful products, including Google Maps and Gmail. Google also has a strong focus on experimentation and continuous improvement, which is reflected in its "fail fast, fail often" philosophy.

Another example is Amazon, which has a culture that encourages risk-taking and experimentation. Amazon founder Jeff Bezos has famously said, "If you're not failing, you're not innovating enough." Amazon has a decentralized organizational structure that allows teams to work independently and make decisions quickly. This has enabled the company to launch several successful products and services, including Amazon Prime and Amazon Web Services. In contrast, companies that have a culture that discourages innovation may struggle to keep up with changing market conditions and customer demands. These companies may be more focused on maintaining the status quo and avoiding risk, which can lead to missed opportunities and stagnant growth.

Creating a culture of innovation is essential for companies that want to stay competitive and grow over the long term. This requires a commitment to providing resources and support for innovation, as well as establishing a mindset that values creativity and risk-taking. Companies that are successful in creating a culture of innovation are often those that are willing to challenge the status quo, embrace change, and continuously improve. As we have already seen, innovation can come from anywhere within an organization, so it's important to encourage and empower all employees, regardless of position or importance, to contribute their ideas. Additionally, companies should be open to collaboration with external partners and customers to bring fresh perspectives and insights into their innovation process.

CHAPTER V

Product Life Cycle & Innovation Diffusion

The Product Life Cycle

The product life cycle is a conceptual model that describes the stages a product goes through from its initial introduction to the market until its eventual decline and obsolescence. The model is typically depicted as a bell curve, with four main stages: introduction, growth, maturity, and decline.

During the introduction stage, a new product is launched into the market, and sales are typically slow as consumers become aware of its existence. The growth stage is characterized by increasing sales as the product gains popularity and becomes more widely known. In the maturity stage, sales growth slows down as the product reaches market saturation, and the competition intensifies. Finally, in the decline stage, sales decline as the product becomes less popular or is replaced by newer and better products.

The product life cycle concept is useful for businesses in terms of planning and managing their product strategies. Understanding where a product is in its life cycle can help a company decide whether to invest in further development, modify its marketing strategy, or discontinue the product altogether. Additionally, companies can use the product life cycle model to predict future sales and plan accordingly.

Diffusion of Innovation

Diffusion of Innovation is a theory that seeks to explain how, why, and at what rate new ideas and technology spread through cultures. It provides a framework for understanding how innovation is adopted by people and organizations over time. The theory was first introduced by Everett Rogers in his book "Diffusion of Innovations" in 1962. Rogers was a professor of communication studies at the University of New Mexico and a sociologist.

Rogers' theory built upon the work of earlier researchers such as Gabriel Tarde and Bryce Ryan, who explored the spread of new ideas and technologies in society. Rogers defined innovation as an idea, practice, or object that is perceived as new by an individual or other unit of adoption. He proposed that the diffusion of innovation occurs through a five-step process: knowledge, persuasion, decision, implementation, and confirmation. Rogers' key ideas include the importance of communication and social networks in the spread of new ideas, the role of opinion leaders and early adopters in the diffusion process, and the significance of the perceived attributes of the innovation (relative advantage, compatibility, complexity, trialability, and observability) in shaping its adoption.

Since Rogers' original work, other researchers and scholars have built upon and expanded his ideas, including Geoffrey Moore with his "Crossing the Chasm" framework and Everett Rogers himself with his later book "Diffusion of Innovations, 5th Edition."

The diffusion of innovation is related to the product life cycle in that it explains the different stages that a product goes through from introduction to decline. During the introduction stage, innovators are the first to adopt the new product, and they are followed by early adopters during the growth stage. The early majority and late majority adopt the product during the maturity stage, and laggards adopt it during the decline stage.

The diffusion of innovation theory explains how innovations spread through a population and how they are adopted by different groups. The product life cycle explains the different stages that a product goes through in the market. The two theories are related because they both seek to explain how products are adopted and how they become popular or decline in the marketplace.

Perceived Attributes of an Innovation

The perceived attributes of an innovation are the characteristics or features of an innovation that are perceived by potential adopters, and that influence their decision to adopt or reject the innovation. The perceived attributes of an innovation were identified by Everett Rogers as part of the diffusion of innovations theory.

The five perceived attributes of an innovation are:

1. **Relative Advantage:** The degree to which an innovation is perceived as being better than the existing solution or alternative. For example, when smartphones were introduced, they were perceived as having a relative advantage over feature phones because they provided more functionality, such as internet access, touch screens, and applications.

2. **Compatibility:** The degree to which an innovation is perceived as being consistent with the values, experiences, and needs of potential adopters. For example, the adoption of electric cars has been slow because they are perceived as being less compatible with the infrastructure and habits of drivers, such as range anxiety and the need for charging stations.

3. **Complexity:** The degree to which an innovation is perceived as being difficult to understand or use. For example, many people find virtual reality technology complex to use because it requires additional hardware and software to be set up.

4. **Trialability:** The degree to which an innovation can be experimented with or tested before making a decision to adopt or reject it. For example, software companies often provide free trial versions of their products to potential customers to enable them to test and evaluate the product before purchasing it.

5. **Observability:** The degree to which the results or benefits of an innovation are visible to others. For example, the adoption of renewable energy technologies such as solar panels can be

influenced by the observability of their use and benefits, such as cost savings and environmental impact.

These five perceived attributes influence the diffusion of innovations and the rate of adoption of a new product or service in the market. Innovations that are perceived as having high relative advantage, compatibility, trialability, and observability, and low complexity, are more likely to be adopted by potential customers.

Product Adoption and Adopter Categories

Once a product is launched, not everybody goes out and buys it immediately. Research has shown that the adoption of products follows a distinctive pattern. Certain types of customers are first to buy, while others jump on the bandwagon later. In general, the categories of adopters in the marketplace are:

1. **Innovators (2.5% of the market):** Innovators are the first to adopt a new product or service. They are willing to take risks and are highly knowledgeable about new technology. They are usually well off and are willing to pay a premium price to try out a new product.

2. **Early Adopters (13.5% of the market):** Early adopters are those who adopt a new product or service after the innovators. They are opinion leaders and often have a significant influence on the rest of the market.

3. **Early Majority (34% of the market):** The early majority are those who adopt a new product or service in the early stages of its

mass-market availability. They are deliberate in their adoption and tend to do more research and consider more options than early adopters.

4. **Late Majority (34% of the market):** The late majority are those who adopt a new product or service after the early majority. They are more skeptical and conservative in their decision-making, and may adopt a new product only when it becomes the norm.

5. **Laggards (16% of the market):** Laggards are the last to adopt a new product or service. They are typically older, less educated, and more traditional in their values and beliefs. They are also motivated heavily by price.

Adoption Category	Description	Example
Innovators	First to adopt, willing to take risks	First doctors to use a new medical device
Early Adopters	Next to adopt, opinion leaders	Farmers trying organic techniques
Early Majority	Adopt after seeing success with early adopters	Stores adding self-checkout lanes
Late Majority	Adopt after majority have embraced the product	Seniors signing up for Facebook
Laggards	Last to adopt, skeptical of change	Engineers clinging to manual drafting tools

Table: Adoption Categories with Examples

According to the theory of the diffusion of innovations, new goods and services are adopted by customers in a consistent pattern over the course of time, and this pattern in turn is connected to the product life cycle.

During the course of a product's life cycle, it can go from being unheard of to being adopted by a large number of people. During various points of the product's life cycle, different groups of consumers are likely to embrace the product. The product is most likely to be adopted by innovators and early adopters during the growth and introduction stages. Once it has reached these groups, the product is adopted next by the early majority and late majority, as it gets relatively mature. In the event that they purchase the product at all, laggards do so during the decline phase. When marketers have an understanding of the many types of adopters and the behaviors that characterize each category, they are better able to develop tailored marketing strategies for each group, which in turn helps to maximize the success of the product.

Typical Pain Points

Here are some examples of pain points that customers may face when adopting a new product:

1. **Learning curve:** Customers may struggle to understand how to use the new product, especially if it has a complex interface or requires significant changes in behavior.

2. **Compatibility issues:** The new product may not work well with other products that the customer already owns, such as different operating systems, software programs, or hardware.

3. **Performance problems:** The new product may not perform as expected, or it may have technical issues that cause frustration and decrease its value.

4. **Cost:** The cost of the new product may be too high, or there may be hidden costs associated with its use, such as subscription fees or maintenance costs.

5. **Risk:** Customers may perceive that the new product poses some risk, such as security or privacy concerns, or that they may suffer financial losses if the product fails.

6. **Support:** Customers may feel that they are not receiving adequate support from the company, such as poor customer service or a lack of training resources.

7. **Perception of need:** Customers may not see the need for the new product, or they may feel that it does not solve a significant problem for them.

Due to some of these pain points, customers may choose to postpone their transition to the new offering or even give up on it entirely. To improve their chances of widespread adoption and sustained expansion, businesses need to take the initiative to overcome the problems identified above.

How to Overcome Barriers to Adoption

The success of a new product is highly dependent on customers' understanding and willingness to adopt it. In a world where customers are bombarded with information, it is essential for both startups and established firms to invest in marketing and educate potential customers on their product's value proposition. Testimonials, usage details, and ROI examples can help convince customers to make a purchase.

Adopting a new product can also be difficult for customers, especially if it requires a change in behavior or involves multiple decision-makers. Firms must focus on selling to each of the constituents in the sales chain and recognize that this may take more time and resources. Additionally, high direct and indirect costs, potential risk, and new pain points can make customers hesitant to adopt a new product. After initial adoption, businesses must also consider obstacles that can cause sales to decline or usage to stop. These include the lagging support infrastructure, new pain points, and products that are incorrectly targeted. Inadequate attention to these obstacles is a primary reason why many newly launched products fail to meet growth and revenue projections.

While innovative solutions are important, targeting and appealing to the right customers and jobs that they need done is equally critical for success. Launching a product without doing prior work on understanding the target market, or developing a proper segmentation strategy can backfire even if the product itself is capable. A customer-centric approach can help overcome the obstacles to product adoption and long-term growth.

Adoption of Services

The stages of new service adoption are similar to those of new product adoption and can be broken down into the following:

1. **Awareness:** The customer becomes aware of the new service and its benefits.

2. **Interest:** The customer becomes interested in the new service and begins to seek more information.

3. **Evaluation:** The customer evaluates the new service and compares it to their current options.

4. **Trial:** The customer tries the new service on a small scale to see if it meets their needs.

5. **Adoption:** The customer adopts the new service and begins using it on a regular basis.

To accelerate the adoption of new services, several tactics can be used:

1. **Create awareness:** Increase visibility of the new service through advertising, social media, and other promotional channels.

2. **Provide education:** Educate potential customers on the benefits of the new service and how it can help them.

3. **Offer incentives:** Provide incentives to encourage customers to try the new service, such as free trials or discounts.

4. **Target early adopters:** Focus marketing efforts on early adopters who are more likely to try new services and provide positive feedback.

5. **Address pain points:** Address any concerns or obstacles that may prevent customers from adopting the new service.

6. **Monitor feedback:** Monitor customer feedback and make adjustments to the service based on their feedback to ensure a positive experience.

By implementing these tactics, businesses can help accelerate the adoption of new services and increase their chances of success in the market.

Example: Launching Uber

When Uber launched in San Francisco in 2010, they faced regulatory challenges and fierce competition from established taxi services. To overcome these challenges, they used a strategy of offering high-quality, reliable service to early adopters and building a loyal customer base through word-of-mouth marketing. They focused on providing a seamless and efficient experience for customers by using GPS technology to locate and dispatch nearby drivers, offering in-app payment options, and providing riders with real-time updates on their driver's location and estimated arrival time. Additionally, they implemented surge pricing during peak times to incentivize more drivers to hit the road, which helped them maintain consistent wait times and reliable service.

In addition, in order to promote awareness and interest in the service, Uber offered free rides to new users and provided existing users with an incentive to suggest their friends by means of a referral program. Because of this, they were able to establish a solid foundation of early adopters who were open to experimenting with a brand new and cutting-edge service.

Thanks to these techniques, Uber was able to rapidly expand to additional locations and create considerable first-time sales. This was also helped by the company's aggressive marketing, as well as coverage it received in the popular media (both good and bad). By the end of 2010, they had already completed their one millionth journey and had expanded their operations to New York City and Paris. By the end of 2011, they were operating in 16 different cities and had reached daily gross bookings of more than one million dollars. The company's initial launch phase success can be attributed to its focus on delivering a service that is of a high quality and reliable, using cutting-edge technology and marketing strategies to generate buzz and interest in the service, and building a customer base that is loyal through word-of-mouth marketing.

Product Management Resources

1. Product Development and Management Association (PDMA) - https://www.pdma.org/

2. ProductPlan - https://www.productplan.com/

3. Mind the Product - https://www.mindtheproduct.com/

4. Product Hunt - https://www.producthunt.com/

5. Product Manager HQ - https://www.productmanagerhq.com/

CHAPTER VI

Collaborative Innovation

Collaborative innovation refers to the process of innovating through partnerships and collaborations between different individuals, organizations, or institutions. This approach to innovation involves sharing knowledge, expertise, resources, and risks to create new products, services, or processes that would be difficult or impossible to achieve alone.

There are several types of collaborative arrangements that can be formed for innovation, including:

1. **Strategic alliances:** These are partnerships between two or more organizations that agree to share resources and knowledge to achieve a common goal. Strategic alliances can be formed for a specific project or a long-term collaboration. This type of collaborative arrangement can be beneficial for organizations looking to enter new markets, reduce costs, or access new technologies. However, strategic alliances can be difficult to

manage and may lead to conflicts over control, intellectual property, and other issues.

2. **Joint ventures:** These are collaborations between two or more organizations that create a separate legal entity to undertake a specific project or business venture. Joint ventures involve sharing ownership, risks, and profits. This type of collaborative arrangement can provide access to new markets and resources, and can allow organizations to share risks and costs. However, joint ventures can be complex to set up and manage, and can lead to conflicts over control and decision-making.

3. **Consortia:** These are groups of organizations that come together to undertake a specific research or development project. Consortia are typically formed around a shared interest or industry. This type of collaborative arrangement can allow organizations to share resources and expertise, and can facilitate collaboration and knowledge-sharing within an industry or sector. However, consortia can be difficult to manage and may lead to conflicts over intellectual property and other issues.

4. **Open innovation:** This approach involves using external ideas, technologies, and resources to complement internal innovation efforts. Open innovation can be achieved through partnerships, crowdsourcing, or other collaborative arrangements. This type of collaborative arrangement can allow organizations to access a wider range of ideas and resources, and can facilitate collaboration with external partners. However, open innovation can require a significant investment of time and resources to

identify and manage external partners, and may lead to conflicts over ownership and intellectual property.

5. **Co-creation:** This involves collaborating with customers, suppliers, or other stakeholders to develop new products or services. Co-creation involves involving external partners in the innovation process from the outset. This type of collaborative arrangement can allow organizations to gain valuable insights into customer needs and preferences, and can facilitate collaboration and innovation with external partners. However, co-creation can be difficult to manage and may require a high level of coordination and communication with external partners, and may also lead to conflicts over ownership and intellectual property.

6. **Licensing agreements:** Licensing agreements involve one company granting another company the right to use its intellectual property, such as patents, trademarks, or copyrights, in exchange for royalties or other forms of compensation. Licensing agreements are often used to leverage existing technologies or products.

7. **Research and development (R&D) partnerships:** R&D partnerships involve two or more companies collaborating on research and development activities, such as developing new technologies or conducting clinical trials. R&D partnerships allow companies to share resources, knowledge, and expertise to accelerate innovation.

8. **Supply chain partnerships:** Supply chain partnerships involve companies collaborating to optimize their supply chain operations, such as improving efficiency, reducing costs, or enhancing sustainability. Supply chain partnerships can involve suppliers, manufacturers, distributors, and retailers working together to improve the entire supply chain ecosystem.

Collaboration Type	Companies Involved	Year	Key Objectives
Joint Venture	Dow Corning	1943	Commercialize silicone products
Strategic Alliance	Starbucks and Spotify	2015	Enhance in-store music
Technology Licensing	Microsoft and Samsung	2005	Access to Microsoft patents
Consortium	AAMA (Toyota, Ford, GM)	1915	Standardize vehicle parts
Co-Marketing	Uber and Spotify	2016	Cross-promote apps
Equity Strategic Partnership	Intel and Cloudera	2014	Expand big data solutions
Supply Chain Partnership	Unilever and Walmart	2009	Sustainability initiatives
Consortia	W3C (Apple, Google, Amazon, etc)	1994	Develop web standards

Table. Collaborative Innovation Examples

Overall, collaborative innovation is a powerful tool for organizations to create new and innovative products, services, or processes. By working together, organizations can leverage each other's strengths and resources to achieve outcomes that would be difficult or impossible to achieve alone.

Alliances Require Careful Due Diligence

The term 'strategic alliance' can be used very broadly, including to refer to one of the other forms of collaboration outlined above, e.g. joint venture. The points below refer to all forms of collaboration which involve an alliance between two partner companies. Before forming a strategic alliance, the companies in question should conduct thorough due diligence to ensure that the partnership is a good fit and has the potential to be successful. Here are some criteria and due diligence to consider:

1. **Strategic fit:** The alliance should be aligned with the long-term strategic goals of both companies. Companies should assess whether the partnership will help them achieve their objectives, such as entering new markets, developing new products, or expanding their customer base.

2. **Compatibility:** The two companies should have compatible cultures, values, and management styles. Companies should assess whether the partnership is a good cultural fit and whether there are any potential conflicts or challenges that could arise.

3. **Complementary strengths:** The two companies should have complementary strengths and capabilities that will allow them to create a unique value proposition. Companies should assess whether their products, services, and expertise complement each other, and whether there are any gaps that need to be addressed.

4. **Financial viability:** Companies should assess the financial viability of the partnership, including the potential costs, risks,

and returns. Companies should conduct a thorough financial analysis, including assessing the potential revenue streams, the expected costs, and the potential return on investment.

5. **Legal and regulatory considerations:** Companies should assess the legal and regulatory considerations associated with the partnership, including any licensing, intellectual property, or regulatory issues that could arise. Companies should ensure that they have the legal expertise to address any issues that may arise.

6. **Governance and decision-making:** Companies should establish a clear governance structure and decision-making process for the partnership. Companies should ensure that there are clear roles and responsibilities, and that decision-making is transparent and fair.

7. **Exit strategy:** Companies should establish an exit strategy in case the partnership does not work out as planned. Companies should consider potential risks and liabilities associated with the partnership, and establish a plan for how to manage these risks in the event that the partnership is dissolved.

From Alliances to Mergers

Strategic alliances often involve companies collaborating and working closely together, which can create opportunities for them to explore deeper levels of integration and potentially merge to form a single entity. In some cases, strategic alliances may be seen as a precursor to a merger, allowing companies to test the waters of collaboration before committing to a full merger.

However, several factors can eventually influence mergers, including:

1. **Synergies:** Mergers may be driven by the desire to achieve synergies, such as cost savings, improved efficiency, or increased market power. By merging, companies can combine their resources, capabilities, and expertise to create a more powerful and competitive entity.

2. **Market conditions:** Mergers may be influenced by broader market conditions, such as changes in customer preferences, technological disruptions, or regulatory changes. Companies may look to merge in order to respond to these changes or to take advantage of new opportunities in the market.

3. **Financial considerations:** Mergers may be driven by financial considerations, such as the desire to improve profitability, access new sources of capital, or diversify revenue streams. By merging, companies may be able to achieve economies of scale, reduce costs, or generate new revenue streams.

4. **Strategic considerations:** Mergers may also be driven by strategic considerations, such as the desire to enter new markets, expand product offerings, position against specific competitors, or acquire new technologies or intellectual property. By merging with another company, a company may be able to gain access to new resources and capabilities that it would not have been able to achieve on its own.

5. **Cultural fit:** Mergers can be complex and challenging, and a key factor in their success is often the cultural fit between the two

companies. Companies may look for mergers with partners that share similar values, leadership styles, and organizational cultures to minimize the risk of post-merger integration challenges.

Merger activity in any industry can vary from year to year, and can be influenced by broader economic and social factors. For example, the state of merger and alliance activity in 2021 was marked by a significant increase as companies looked to position themselves for growth and resilience in the face of the COVID-19 pandemic and other economic challenges. According to data from Refinitiv, global merger and acquisition activity surged in the first half of 2021, reaching its highest level in over two decades. The total value of deals announced in the first half of 2021 was $2.4 trillion, up 131% from the same period in 2020. The technology, healthcare, and energy sectors were among the most active in terms of deal-making.

In addition to mergers and acquisitions, there was also a trend towards strategic alliances and partnerships in 2021. Many companies were seeking to collaborate on innovation and digital transformation initiatives, as well as to access new markets and customers. For example, in 2021, Amazon and Ford announced a partnership to integrate Alexa, Amazon's voice assistant, into Ford vehicles.

The COVID-19 pandemic also accelerated the trend towards digitalization and remote work, which in turn led to increased collaboration and partnerships in the technology sector. Companies were seeking to leverage each other's expertise and technologies to develop new solutions for remote work, online learning, and other areas.

This overall high level of merger and alliance activity was focused on growth and resilience in the face of economic challenges.

Merger Case: Higher Education Sector

To look at an instructive case of a merger that took many years to come to fruition, one can look at an example from the educational sector.

The Brooklyn Polytechnic Institute was established in 1854 in Brooklyn, New York as the Brooklyn Collegiate and Polytechnic Institute. In 1921, the school was renamed to Brooklyn Polytechnic Institute, and in 1985 it was renamed again to Polytechnic University (but was still commonly referred to as Brooklyn Poly). Polytechnic University eventually merged with New York University (NYU) in 2008. The merger process took several years to complete and involved several key steps:

1. **Exploratory discussions:** The idea of a merger was first proposed in the early 2000s, when NYU and Brooklyn Poly began holding exploratory discussions about the potential benefits of a partnership.

2. **Feasibility study:** In 2004, NYU and Brooklyn Poly commissioned a feasibility study to assess the potential benefits and challenges of a merger. The study included input from faculty, staff, students, and alumni, and concluded that a merger could create a stronger, more competitive institution.

3. **Negotiations:** Following the feasibility study, NYU and Brooklyn Poly began formal negotiations to develop a merger agreement. The negotiations included discussions about financial terms, governance, and academic programs.

4. **Approval process:** Once a merger agreement was reached, it was subject to approval by various governing bodies, including the boards of trustees of both institutions, the New York State Education Department, and accrediting agencies.

5. **Integration planning:** In the years leading up to the official merger, NYU and Brooklyn Poly began planning for the integration of the two institutions. This involved developing plans for academic programs, facilities, and administrative functions, as well as addressing issues related to culture and identity.

6. **Merger completion:** The merger was officially completed on January 1, 2008, when Brooklyn Poly became part of NYU's Tandon School of Engineering. The merged institution was renamed the NYU Tandon School of Engineering.

Overall, the merger process between Brooklyn Poly and NYU took several years to complete and involved a complex series of steps, negotiations, and approvals. There is of course no set time frame for the completion of mergers. There have been many instances in corporate America of mergers that take place within weeks or months.

Corporate Acquisitions

Acquisitions refer to the process of one company purchasing another company's assets, stocks, or ownership stake in order to gain control over it. There are several types of corporate acquisitions, including:

1. **Horizontal acquisition:** This occurs when one company acquires another company that operates in the same industry and market as the acquiring company. An example of a horizontal acquisition is Facebook's acquisition of Instagram, which allowed Facebook to expand its social media offerings and gain access to Instagram's user base.

2. **Vertical acquisition:** This type of acquisition involves a company acquiring a business that is either a supplier or a customer of the acquiring company. An example of a vertical acquisition is Amazon's acquisition of Whole Foods, which allowed Amazon to integrate its online retail platform with Whole Foods' brick-and-mortar stores.

3. **Conglomerate acquisition:** This occurs when a company acquires another company that operates in a completely different industry or market. An example of a conglomerate acquisition is Berkshire Hathaway's acquisition of Dairy Queen, which is a fast-food restaurant chain that operates in a completely different industry than Berkshire Hathaway's other holdings.

Corporate acquisitions are different from mergers in that mergers occur when two companies agree to combine their assets, stocks, or ownership stakes in order to form a new company. In a merger, both companies typically have equal say in the management and decision-making of the new company, whereas in an acquisition, the acquiring company takes control of the acquired company. Acquisitions can be friendly or hostile, and they are often used as a growth strategy by companies looking to expand their market share, diversify their offerings, or gain access to new technologies or resources. Acquisitions are generally financed through cash payments, stock swaps, or a combination of both.

CHAPTER VII

Protecting Innovation

A Cornerstone of Competitive Advantage

While it is one thing to create and drive innovation, it is equally important to think about how the firm can benefit from it in the long run. As Michael Porter argues in his book "Competitive Advantage", effective intellectual property protection can be a critical element of a firm's overall competitive strategy. It is therefore important to have a strategy to protect innovation for several reasons. As we shall see, there are also situations where the decision may be to not protect innovation. Either way, there should be a strong strategic consideration and rationale behind these decisions.

There is no question that innovation has the potential to be a primary driver of both the competitiveness and profitability of a company. If proper protection is not provided to the innovations being generated, it is possible that other companies will be able to readily replicate or imitate the innovation(s), which will result in a loss of market share as well as a reduction in profits. In addition, we already know that considerable investments of both time and resources are typically required for innovation. In the absence of proper protection, it is possible for competitors to free-ride on the expenditures made by the company that is inventing. This can result in an unfair advantage and lower incentives for continued innovation. Protection can provide a legal framework to enforce the innovating firm's intellectual property rights, allowing the innovating firm to take legal action against parties who infringe on those rights. This is particularly important for innovations that have required a significant investment of resources, such as a new molecule that creates a breakthrough drug.

Finally, a powerful innovation protection plan can also boost a company's brand and credibility, which is especially important in fields that place a premium on intellectual property's ownership and protection. Protection can also make it easier for companies to collaborate and enter licensing agreements with one another, which gives the owner of the intellectual property the opportunity to earn additional revenue streams and increase its presence in the market.

Strategies for Protecting Innovation

There are several standard strategies for protecting innovation, including:

1. **Patents:** A patent is a legal protection that gives the inventor the exclusive right to make, use, and sell their invention for a certain period of time. Patents can be granted for a wide range of innovations, including processes, machines, and designs.

2. **Trademarks:** A trademark is a symbol, design, word, or phrase that is used to identify and distinguish a company's products or services from those of others. It can be protected through registration and use in commerce.

3. **Copyrights:** A copyright protects original works of authorship, such as literary, musical, or artistic creations. It gives the author the exclusive right to reproduce, distribute, and display their work.

4. **Trade secrets:** A trade secret is a confidential piece of information that gives a company a competitive advantage. It can include things like customer lists, manufacturing processes, and formulas.

Some other methods include:

1. **Industrial design rights:** Industrial design rights protect the visual design of a product, such as its shape, configuration, pattern, or ornamentation.

2. **Plant variety protection:** A form of intellectual property protection for new varieties of plants that are distinct, uniform, and stable. Typically these plants offer specific benefits like resistance to pests or higher yields and are therefore deemed worthy of protection.

3. **Geographical indications:** Geographical indications are used to identify products that originate from a specific geographic location and have certain qualities or characteristics due to that

location, such as sparkling wine from the Champagne region of France.

The following table lists these different types of protection along with specific examples:

Type of Protection	Example	Year	Description
Patents	iPhone	2007	Apple was granted numerous patents related to the design, technology, and functionality of the iPhone. This allowed them to exclude competitors from making, using, or selling similar devices.
Trademarks	Coca-Cola	1892	Coca-Cola's trademark protects its iconic brand name, logo, and red-and-white color scheme, allowing the company to prevent others from using similar marks that could cause confusion in the marketplace.
Copyrights	Harry Potter and the Philosopher's Stone	1997	J.K. Rowling's copyright protected her original literary work, preventing others from copying or distributing the book without her permission.
Trade Secrets	KFC Recipe	N/A	KFC's secret recipe for its famous fried chicken is a trade secret, giving the company a competitive advantage by keeping the recipe confidential and preventing others from replicating it.
Industrial Design Rights	Dyson Airblade	2006	Dyson's industrial design rights protect the distinctive shape and configuration of its Airblade hand dryer, preventing competitors from copying its design.
Plant Variety Protection	Honeycrisp Apples	1991	The Honeycrisp apple variety was granted plant variety protection, allowing its developers to control the commercial use of the variety for a certain period of time.
Geographical Indications	Champagne	N/A	Champagne is a protected geographical indication, meaning that only sparkling wine produced in the Champagne region of France can be labeled and sold as "Champagne."

Table: Innovation Protection Examples

The pros of protecting innovation include:

1. **Encouraging innovation:** By protecting innovation, inventors and companies are incentivized to invest in research and development, knowing that they will be able to reap the rewards of their work.

2. **Competitive advantage:** Protecting innovation can give a company a competitive advantage by preventing others from copying their inventions or ideas.

3. **Revenue generation:** Companies can license or sell their patents or trademarks to generate revenue.

The cons of protecting innovation include:

1. **Costs:** Obtaining and enforcing patents, trademarks, and copyrights can be expensive and time-consuming.

2. **Stifling innovation:** Some argue that overly restrictive intellectual property laws can actually stifle innovation by preventing others from building upon existing ideas.

3. **Limited lifespan:** Patents and trademarks have a limited lifespan, after which the invention or trademark becomes part of the public domain.

Patent-Granting Organizations

In the United States, the United States Patent and Trademark Office (USPTO) is the federal agency responsible for granting patents and registering trademarks. Its role is to examine patent applications and determine whether an invention is eligible for patent protection under US law. The USPTO also provides resources for inventors, businesses, and the public to learn about intellectual property rights and the patent process. The USPTO has granted patents for some major technological breakthroughs, including:

1. **The Telephone (1876)** - The patent for the telephone was granted to Alexander Graham Bell on March 7, 1876. The invention revolutionized communication, enabling people to talk to each other over long distances.

2. **The Light Bulb (1879)** - The patent for the incandescent light bulb was granted to Thomas Edison on January 27, 1880. The

invention transformed the world by providing affordable and efficient lighting to homes and businesses.

3. **The Personal Computer (1981)** - The patent for the first personal computer was granted to IBM on August 12, 1981. The invention led to the democratization of computing power, enabling individuals to have access to powerful computing tools and revolutionizing many industries.

4. **The Chiron Corporation patent: In** the late 1980s, the Chiron Corporation was granted a patent for the hepatitis C virus (HCV), which allowed them to develop a diagnostic test for the virus. This patent was significant because it led to the development of treatments for HCV, which had previously been difficult to diagnose and treat.

5. **The BRCA gene patents:** In the 1990s, Myriad Genetics obtained patents on the BRCA1 and BRCA2 genes, which are linked to an increased risk of breast and ovarian cancer. These patents allowed Myriad to have exclusive rights to test for these genes, which caused controversy in the medical community and led to legal challenges.

6. **CRISPR gene-editing technology:** This technology was developed by Jennifer Doudna and Emmanuelle Charpentier, who were awarded the Nobel Prize in Chemistry in 2020. Their groundbreaking work on CRISPR, which allows for precise and efficient gene editing, has been the subject of several patents

Other countries have similar agencies to the USPTO. For example, the European Patent Office (EPO) is responsible for granting European patents and the Japan Patent Office (JPO) is responsible for granting patents in Japan.

In addition to national patent offices, there are also international organizations that work to promote intellectual property protection and harmonization of patent laws among different countries. For example, the World Intellectual Property Organization (WIPO) is a specialized agency of the United Nations that works to promote and protect intellectual property rights worldwide. The WIPO administers a number of international treaties related to patents, including the Patent Cooperation Treaty (PCT), which allows inventors to seek patent protection in multiple countries through a single international application process.

A corporation with a US patent would need to apply to other patent offices in other markets if they wish to protect their invention in those markets. This is because patents are granted on a country-by-country basis, and a US patent only provides protection in the United States.

The process of applying for a patent in another country can be time-consuming and expensive. Each country has its own patent laws and procedures, which means that the application process can differ significantly from country to country. In general, the process involves filing a separate application in each country where the applicant wishes to obtain patent protection. This can be a complex and expensive process, as each application may need to be translated into the local language, and fees must be paid for each application.

Additionally, the timeline for obtaining a patent can vary greatly depending on the country. Some countries have faster and more streamlined processes, while others may take several years to complete. The cost of obtaining a patent can also vary greatly depending on the country and the complexity of the invention. In some cases, it may cost tens of thousands of dollars to obtain a patent in a single country. As a result, a number of companies with a high output of IP frequently employ large teams of lawyers, both internally and externally.

Acquiring a Trademark

To obtain a trademark in the United States, one must also file an application with the United States Patent and Trademark Office (USPTO). The application must include the specific word, phrase, symbol, design, or combination thereof that is being claimed as a trademark, as well as the goods or services associated with the trademark. Trademarks protect any word, name, symbol, or device, or any combination thereof, used by a person or entity to identify and distinguish their goods or services from those of others. This includes company names, logos, product names, slogans, and other identifiers used to distinguish a brand from its competitors. The table below shows some examples of trademarks granted to some recent companies. While most of these are smaller companies by revenues and market share, some have garnered a lot of attention due to their rapid growth and impact.

Trademark	Year Granted	Product/Service
Yeti	2007	Coolers, drinkware
Peloton	2014	Exercise equipment
Waze	2009	Navigation app
Squarespace	2005	Website builder
Glossier	2014	Beauty products
Casper	2013	Mattresses, bedding
Rent the Runway	2009	Clothing rental
Ring	2012	Smart doorbells
Houzz	2008	Home design platform
Curology	2014	Customized skincare

Table. Examples of Trademarks

Trademarks are enforceable by law, and the owner of a registered trademark can take legal action against anyone who infringes on their trademark rights. Infringement occurs when someone uses a mark that is confusingly similar to an existing trademark, which can cause consumer confusion and dilute the value of the original mark.

Some famous trademarks of more established companies include Nike's "swoosh" logo, Apple's bitten apple logo, Coca-Cola's logo, McDonald's golden arches, and Google's multi-colored logo.

Copyrights

To obtain a copyright, an individual or entity must create an original work of authorship fixed in a tangible medium of expression, such as a book, song, film, or software code. The copyright automatically protects the work from the moment it is created, but registration with the U.S. Copyright Office is recommended to provide additional legal benefits.

Copyright protection generally extends to the expression of ideas, rather than the ideas themselves. It gives the owner exclusive rights to reproduce, distribute, display, perform, and create derivative works based on the original work. These rights can be licensed or sold to others, allowing the copyright owner to profit from their creation. Copyright is enforceable through legal action, including seeking injunctions to stop infringement and damages for losses suffered as a result of the infringement. However, the cost of enforcing a copyright can be high, and it can be difficult to prove infringement, especially in the case of digital works.

Some famous examples of copyrighted works include literary works like the Harry Potter series by J.K. Rowling, musical works like Michael Jackson's "Thriller," and visual works like Leonardo da Vinci's "Mona Lisa."

Trade Secrets

Trade secrets are confidential information that a business has and uses to gain a competitive advantage in the market. Examples of trade secrets include formulas, processes, designs, customer lists, and marketing strategies. Unlike patents or trademarks, trade secrets do not require any registration or filing with government agencies. Instead, they are protected through a combination of legal and technological means, such as non-disclosure agreements, access controls, and employee training programs.

To obtain trade secret protection, businesses need to take reasonable steps to keep their information secret and limit access to it. This includes implementing security measures, such as password protection, encryption, and physical barriers, as well as requiring employees and contractors to sign non-disclosure agreements.

Trade secret protection is enforceable through legal action if someone breaches the confidentiality agreement or misuses the confidential information. Remedies for trade secret theft may include injunctions, damages, and, in some cases, criminal penalties.

Famous examples of trade secrets include the formula for Coca-Cola, the recipe for KFC's fried chicken, and the algorithms used by search engines like Google.

Appropriability versus Diffusion

In the context of innovation, "appropriability" refers to a company's ability to retain the economic benefits of an innovation, while "diffusion" refers to the spread of the innovation beyond the company to other individuals or organizations. The tradeoff between these two concepts is that the more a company seeks to appropriate the benefits of an innovation, the less it is likely to diffuse and be adopted by others. On the other hand, the more an innovation diffuses, the less likely a company is to directly appropriate its benefits.

Appropriability and diffusion are important considerations in innovation strategy, as they determine how much control a company has over the innovation and how much benefit it can derive from it. On one hand, if a company chooses to keep its innovations wholly proprietary, it may enjoy greater control over their use and may be able to capture more value from them. However, this approach also limits the potential diffusion of the innovation and may result in missed opportunities for collaboration and partnership. However, if a company chooses to adopt a wholly open innovation approach, it may benefit from increased diffusion and collaboration, but may also risk losing control over the innovation and may find it difficult to capture value from it.

Prominent examples of companies that have adopted different positions on the appropriability-diffusion continuum include Apple, which has historically focused on keeping its innovations proprietary, and Google, which has embraced a more open approach to innovation through initiatives like its Android operating system. Another example is the pharmaceutical industry, which has traditionally sought to appropriate the benefits of its innovations through patents and other forms of intellectual property protection, but which is increasingly facing pressure to make its innovations more widely available and accessible.

The Continuum from Closed to Open Innovation

Based on the decisions made about appropriability and diffusion, firms can choose whether to go for a proprietary approach versus a completely open approach. Thus the continuum from wholly proprietary to wholly open innovation refers to the extent to which a company collaborates with external parties in the innovation process. On one end of the continuum, wholly proprietary innovation refers to a closed innovation model where a company develops all new ideas and products internally without seeking external input. This, of course, offers complete protection given that external parties are not privy to the core aspects of the innovation. At the other end of the continuum, wholly open innovation refers to a model where a company collaborates extensively with external partners such as customers, suppliers, and even competitors to co-create new ideas and products.

In practice, most companies fall somewhere in between these two extremes and adopt a hybrid approach that balances internal and external sources of innovation. For example, companies may seek external input in specific areas where they lack expertise or collaborate with suppliers to develop new components for their products.

Prominent examples of wholly proprietary innovation include Apple's development of the iPhone, where the company's engineers and designers worked in secret to develop the product without external input. In contrast, a prominent example of wholly open innovation is the Linux operating system, which was created by a community of developers who shared and collaborated on the code openly without any ownership restrictions.

Open Innovation

Open innovation is a concept introduced by Professor Henry Chesbrough, which describes the process of seeking external sources of innovation and using them in one's own innovation processes, as well as allowing internal ideas to flow out to external partners to bring value to both parties. Chesbrough's work was intended to show that innovation does not always occur within the walls of a company, and that firms that engage in open innovation can better leverage their own ideas and capabilities, as well as tap into the expertise of other firms, customers, and suppliers.

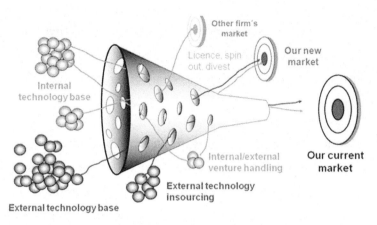

Fig. Open Innovation Paradigm

Source: Henry Chesbrough (2004)

Today, open innovation concepts are widely used by firms to enhance their innovation efforts. Many companies have realized the benefits of collaborating with external partners to develop new products or services, and have adopted open innovation strategies to take advantage of external knowledge and resources. Open innovation has become a strategic tool for firms looking to stay competitive in today's fast-paced and rapidly changing business environment. By embracing open innovation, firms can tap into a much wider pool of ideas, technologies, and expertise, leading to increased creativity, speed, and flexibility in the innovation process.

Open innovation has significant implications in the technology sector, as it changes the way companies approach the development and commercialization of new technologies. Some of the key implications include:

1. **Collaborative Innovation:** Open innovation encourages collaboration and co-creation among companies, customers, and

other external stakeholders. By working together, firms can leverage each other's expertise and resources to develop innovative solutions that meet customer needs and create new markets.

2. **Reduced Costs:** Open innovation can help companies reduce the costs of research and development by sharing the burden of innovation with other organizations. For example, companies can license technology from others, use open-source software, or participate in innovation networks to access external knowledge and expertise.

3. **Increased Flexibility:** Open innovation can help firms respond more quickly to changing market conditions by enabling them to tap into external sources of innovation. Companies can use external resources to develop new products and services, enter new markets, or adapt to new technologies or business models.

4. **Expanded Market Opportunities:** Open innovation can help companies expand their market opportunities by leveraging the resources and expertise of external partners. By partnering with other companies, firms can access new markets, customers, and distribution channels.

5. **Intellectual Property:** Open innovation can also have significant implications for intellectual property (IP) management. Companies must carefully manage their IP rights and determine how much to share with external partners to ensure they

maintain a competitive advantage while still benefiting from collaboration.

Open innovation is thus a powerful tool that can be used to accelerate innovation in the technology sector. By sharing ideas and resources, organizations can reduce costs, increase flexibility, and increase innovation capabilities.

CHAPTER VIII

Market Entry and Timing

What is the Timing of Entry?

Timing of entry refers to the strategic decision of when to enter a market with a new product or service. The timing of entry can have a significant impact on a firm's success in the market, as it can affect the level of competition, the ability to capture market share, and the potential for long-term profitability.

Entering a market too early can be risky, as there may not yet be sufficient demand for the product or the necessary infrastructure may not be in place. However, being a first mover can also offer significant advantages, such as building brand recognition and capturing early market share. Examples of successful first movers include companies like Apple with its iPod, or Amazon with its e-reader, the Kindle. We will explore more details on the first mover advantage in the following section.

Entering a market too late can also be risky, as competitors may have already established strong brand recognition and customer loyalty. However, entering a market later can also offer advantages, such as the ability to learn from the mistakes of early movers and to improve upon their products. Examples of successful late entrants include companies like Google with its search engine and Facebook with its social networking platform.

Overall, the timing of entry into a market is a critical strategic decision for any firm, and requires careful consideration of a range of factors, including the level of competition, customer demand, infrastructure requirements, and potential for long-term profitability.

First Mover Advantage

First mover advantage refers to the benefits that a firm gains by being the first to enter a market. The advantages may include building brand recognition, establishing customer loyalty, securing strategic resources, creating entry barriers, and capturing a dominant market share. Firms can move fast to capitalize on first mover advantage by investing in research and development, building a strong intellectual property portfolio, forging alliances with complementary firms, and aggressively marketing their products or services. They may also seek to establish a technological standard or dominate a key segment of the market.

The barriers for later entrants can be significant. For example, the first mover may have already established a strong brand identity and loyal customer base. They may have also secured key strategic resources, such as exclusive distribution channels or access to specialized expertise. Additionally, the first mover may have patents or other intellectual property that creates high barriers to entry for competitors. Finally, the first mover may have already achieved economies of scale, which can make it difficult for later entrants to compete on price.

The Miles and Snow typology was a framework developed by Raymond E. Miles and Charles C. Snow to classify organizations based on their strategic orientations. The typology suggests that organizations tend to fall into one of four categories: defenders, prospectors, analyzers, or reactors.

1. Defenders are organizations that focus on protecting their existing markets and technologies. They tend to be slow to adapt to new technologies and market opportunities, and often enter new markets after the first movers have established themselves.

2. Prospectors, on the other hand, are organizations that are constantly seeking out new markets and technologies. They are typically the first movers in new markets, and are willing to take risks in order to establish themselves in those markets.

3. Analyzers fall somewhere between defenders and prospectors. They are more cautious than prospectors, but more willing to adapt to new technologies and markets than defenders. They tend to wait and see how new markets develop before entering them.

4. Reactors are organizations that do not have a clear strategic orientation. They tend to be slow to adapt to new technologies and markets, and often enter new markets after the first movers have established themselves.

In terms of timing of entry, prospectors are most likely to be first movers and to capitalize on the advantages that come with that position. Defenders may enter later, but will focus on protecting their existing market share. Analyzers may enter after the initial rush, once they have analyzed the market and identified opportunities for growth. Reactors are likely to enter last, if at all, and may struggle to establish themselves in the market.

Simply being a first mover is not a guarantee of success though. Consider the two examples below. Both firms were first movers; one became a household name, and the other is no longer around:

The classic example of a first mover that was a spectacular success is Amazon, which entered the online retail market in the mid-1990s and established itself as the dominant player in the industry. Amazon's early entry allowed it to build a large customer base and establish brand recognition before competitors entered the market. Additionally, Amazon was able to take advantage of first-mover opportunities, such as expanding its product offerings and creating its own line of electronic devices, like the Kindle and Echo. Today, Amazon is one of the most dominant players in electronic commerce, and is one of the world's strongest brands.

Now consider the case of Webvan, an online grocery delivery company that launched in the late 1990s. Webvan was an online grocery delivery service that aimed to revolutionize the grocery industry by providing customers with the convenience of shopping from home and delivering their orders to their doorsteps. The company operated on a centralized model where they would purchase products from wholesalers, store them in their warehouses, and then deliver them to customers' homes. They built a sophisticated technology infrastructure and distribution network to ensure fast and efficient delivery.

Webvan's business model was built on the assumption that consumers would prefer the convenience of home delivery over the experience of shopping in-store. The company raised more than $800 million in capital and quickly expanded to multiple cities across the United States. However, they faced challenges in scaling their business, including high infrastructure costs and difficulties in managing inventory and delivery logistics. In 2001, the company filed for bankruptcy and shut down all operations.

Although Webvan was ahead of its time in terms of its capabilities, they failed to attract enough customers to sustain its business model.

Another example of a first mover that did not become the market leader is Betamax, a video cassette format introduced by Sony in 1975. Despite being first to market with superior video quality, Betamax ultimately lost out to VHS due to a lack of industry support, limited availability, and higher prices. The Sony-Betamax case is still referred to by veterans of the technology industry.

When a First Mover is the Loser

Although being a first mover in a market can provide a significant advantage, it is not always a guarantee for market leadership. Some conditions where the first mover may still not become the market leader are:

1. **Lack of Resources:** Being first to market requires significant investment in research, development, marketing, and production. A company may not have the necessary resources to sustain its early advantage, allowing later entrants with greater resources to overtake them.

2. **Poor Execution:** Even with a first-mover advantage, a company may fail to execute its strategy effectively. Poor product design, marketing, or distribution can undermine early success and allow competitors to gain market share.

3. **Emerging Technologies:** New technologies and changing customer needs can quickly make early products obsolete, allowing later entrants to capitalize on new opportunities.

4. **Dependence on Complementary Products or Services:** Some products or services are dependent on complementary offerings to succeed. If a first mover fails to secure partnerships or build out the necessary ecosystem, later entrants may be able to leverage their networks to overtake the market leader.

As mentioned earlier, the theory of first mover advantage suggests that the first firm to enter a market can gain significant advantages over its competitors, including brand recognition, customer loyalty, and a head start on product development and market positioning. However, the actual advantages that accrue to first movers may depend on a variety of factors, such as the nature of the innovation, the intensity of competition, and the ability of later entrants to copy or improve upon the original idea.

Company	Launch Date	New Market Leader	Product Type
Myspace	2003	Facebook	Social media
PalmPilot	1996	Apple iPhone	Smartphones
TiVo	1999	Roku	Streaming devices
Friendster	2002	Facebook	Social media
Yahoo	1994	Google	Search engines
Motorola	1973	Nokia	Mobile phones
Blockbuster	1985	Netflix	Rental & streaming
AOL	1989	Google	Internet portal
Kodak	1880s	Canon	Photography
Sears	1886	Amazon	Retail
Pets.com	1998	Chewy	Pet supplies online

Table. Examples of First Movers that Lost

Some studies suggest that early entrants are more likely to succeed in markets where innovation is highly valued, where switching costs for customers are high, or where there are significant network effects that give the first mover a competitive edge. However, other studies suggest something different: they frequently find that later entrants can succeed by learning from the mistakes of the first mover, by taking advantage of new technologies or market trends, or by focusing on niche markets that the first mover may have overlooked. Overall, while the theory of first mover advantage is a useful framework for understanding the strategic dynamics of innovation and competition, it should be applied with caution and in consideration of specific market conditions and industry trends.

CHAPTER IX

Capabilities and Competencies

The Competitive Arena of a Business

A business chooses a specific arena to compete in by analyzing its internal and external environments. This involves assessing its strengths, weaknesses, opportunities, and threats, and then identifying areas where it has a competitive advantage. In order to do this, the firm must carefully calibrate its business-level strategy. In general, business-level strategy involves determining how a company will compete in a specific market or industry.

The objectives of business-level strategy can be classified into four typical forms:

1. **Responding to environmental changes:** The business environment is dynamic and constantly changing, and businesses must be able to adapt to these changes. For example, when smartphones became popular, companies like Apple and Samsung quickly adapted and developed their business strategies

to capitalize on this trend. Thus, adaptation in response to change is a critical component of business-level strategy.

2. **Ensuring approval of functional level strategies:** A business-level strategy should align with the functional-level strategies of different departments and teams within the organization. For example, if a company's business-level strategy is to compete on cost, the functional-level strategies of the finance and production departments must also be aligned to support this objective.

3. **Developing and nurturing potentially valuable capabilities:** These capabilities can include unique skills, resources, and expertise that give the company a competitive advantage. For example, Nike's business-level strategy is to differentiate itself by focusing on product design and innovation, which requires developing and nurturing capabilities in these areas.

4. **Generating sustainable competitive advantage (SCA):** This involves creating a competitive advantage that is difficult for competitors to replicate or imitate. For example, Amazon's business-level strategy is to differentiate itself through its advanced logistics and delivery capabilities, which have created a sustainable competitive advantage in the e-commerce industry.

To achieve these objectives, businesses can pursue specific business-level strategies, including cost leadership, differentiation, focused low-cost, and focused differentiation. Ultimately though, the choice of business-level strategy depends on factors such as the company's resources, capabilities, market position, and competitive environment. By selecting an appropriate strategy and executing it effectively, a business can gain a competitive advantage and achieve its objectives in the chosen arena.

When a firm or a group of firms make above-normal returns, meaning they earn more than their long-run average costs, there are two possible explanations: something to do with the industry in which they operate, or something that the firm owns or controls. The first explanation is related to the external analysis of the industry in which the firm operates, using frameworks like Porter's Five Forces, which we have discussed earlier. These forces include the bargaining power of suppliers and customers, the threat of new entrants and substitute products, and the intensity of rivalry among existing firms. If a firm is able to position itself in an industry where these forces are favorable, it may be able to earn above-normal returns.

The second explanation is related to the internal analysis of the firm, using frameworks like the Resource-Based View (RBV). According to the RBV, a firm's competitive advantage is based on its unique resources and capabilities that are difficult for competitors to imitate. These resources could include physical assets like proprietary technology or intellectual property, as well as intangible assets like brand reputation or organizational culture. If a firm has valuable, rare, inimitable, and non-substitutable resources, it may be able to earn above-normal returns. A more detailed discussion on RBV will be presented in the next chapter.

Creating Value Through Capabilities

The concept of value in business refers to the ability of a firm's capabilities to improve the effectiveness or efficiency of its strategies. The value of a capability is dependent on the type of strategy being pursued. For instance, in a low-cost strategy, the ability to lower costs is crucial for creating value. Timex, a popular watch brand, has been successful in the low-cost market due to its ability to produce affordable watches through efficient production methods and supply chain management. In contrast, a differentiator strategy requires enhancing or premium features to create value. Rolex, a luxury watch brand, has been successful by offering unique features and designs that differentiate it from other watch brands.

To be valuable, a capability must either increase efficiency or effectiveness. Efficiency refers to the ratio of outputs to inputs, while effectiveness refers to the ability to enable new capabilities not previously held. For example, an information system that reduces the number of customer service agents required or increases the number of calls that the same number of agents can answer increases efficiency. On the other hand, opening a new regional campus enables outreach to a new market of students, which increases effectiveness.

Consider these two examples from the airline industry:

- **The Low Cost Approach:** Southwest Airlines has developed several capabilities that enable it to maintain a low-cost structure, including a simplified fleet of aircraft, quick turnaround times at airports, and an efficient point-to-point network. These capabilities allow Southwest to operate with a cost advantage over its competitors, and the firm has consistently been able to achieve above-average returns in the industry.

- **Value through Differentiation:** The UAE based global airline, Emirates, has developed valuable capabilities for its differentiator strategy. Emirates offers a premium service that includes features such as in-flight showers, private suites, and gourmet cuisine. These capabilities enable Emirates to differentiate itself from its competitors and offer a unique value proposition to customers. Emirates has been able to generate above-average returns by attracting high-end customers willing to pay a premium price for its services.

In both the examples above, the capabilities developed by the firms enable them to improve their efficiency and effectiveness in pursuing their respective strategies. By doing so, they are able to create value for their customers and generate above-normal returns for their shareholders. Although they both compete in the same industry, the way they are positioned as individual firms and brands could hardly be more dissimilar.

Hence we can say that firms can create value through capabilities that enable strategies to improve efficiency or effectiveness. The type of strategy pursued determines the type of capabilities that are valuable, and a capability is only valuable if it increases efficiency or effectiveness.

What are Capabilities?

A company's capabilities can be defined as its capacity to carry out a particular action or assignment in a way that is beneficial to the business as a whole. They consist of a company's resources, knowledge, skills, and technology, and they are the combination that enables the company to realize its business objectives. The term "capabilities" can refer to a number of different things, including "research and development," "production," "marketing," "sales," or "customer service."

Capabilities can be further broken down into three primary types: organizational, technical, and management capabilities. The structure, culture, and resources of an organization are referred to as its organizational capabilities. The technical capabilities of an organization encompass specialized apparatus, methods, and procedures. The managerial capabilities of an organization are the managers' and leaders' individual skill sets and bodies of knowledge. These capabilities include the managers' and leaders' capacities to make sound decisions and effectively manage teams.

The Industrial Organizations (IO) View of the Firm

The industrial organization (IO) school of thought posits that firms within an industry have similar strategic resources that are easily transferable between firms. IO scholars focus on the external environment and market forces, such as industry structure, competition, and government regulations. According to this view, a firm's ability to achieve competitive advantage and above-normal returns is determined by the industry's characteristics, rather than the firm's internal resources and capabilities. As we have seen previously, Porter's Five Forces Model belongs to the IO school, where the focus is on external dynamics particularly at the industry level. IO scholars also believe that the behavior of firms is influenced by the degree of market concentration, entry barriers, and the level of product differentiation within an industry, which can affect the level of competition and profitability. However, critics argue that this approach neglects the importance of internal resources and capabilities in shaping a firm's competitive advantage.

Resource-Based View (RBV) of the Firm

The Resource-Based View (RBV) of the firm is a managerial framework that emphasizes the internal *resources and capabilities* of a firm as the primary sources of sustained competitive advantage. The RBV suggests that a firm's unique resources and capabilities, including tangible and intangible assets, intellectual property, organizational processes, and culture, are what create competitive advantage.

The RBV suggests that the value, rarity, inimitability, and non-substitutability of a firm's resources and capabilities are the key determinants of competitive advantage. These resources and capabilities should be exploited strategically to generate sustained superior performance. The framework also suggests that resources and capabilities are not equally important, and that some are more critical than others.

The RBV is different from the traditional Industrial Organization (IO) view, which emphasizes external factors such as market structure, industry forces, and competitive dynamics. The RBV suggests that the internal resources and capabilities of the firm are more important in determining its performance than external factors. The RBV school recognizes that resources are not perfectly mobile between firms and that different firms may have different sets of resources and capabilities that can be leveraged for competitive advantage. For example, Apple's design capabilities, brand image, and innovation culture are difficult to imitate and have allowed the company to achieve a sustained competitive advantage in the technology industry. Similarly, Coca-Cola's strong brand image, distribution network, and marketing capabilities have allowed the company to maintain a dominant position in the soft drink industry despite intense competition. In both cases, the unique resources and capabilities of the firms are the key sources of their competitive advantage, and these resources are not easily transferable between firms. This is what makes these firms iconic and extremely hard to imitate.

CHAPTER X

Towards Sustainable Competitive Advantage

The Path to Sustainable Competitive Advantage (SCA)

Sustainable competitive advantage is the ultimate goal for any company looking to thrive and survive in a competitive market. It is the holy grail of business, the key to long-term success, and the foundation of a winning strategy. To achieve it, a company must have something valuable and unique that sets it apart from its competitors, and that cannot be easily replicated or imitated. As we shall see, it must be a resource or capability that is rare, valuable, inimitable, and organized, and that can be leveraged to create value for customers, generate profits for the company, and maintain a competitive edge in the marketplace. In this chapter, we will explore the concept of sustainable competitive advantage, its importance, and the strategies and tactics that companies can use to achieve and maintain it in a rapidly changing and dynamic business environment. To understand how we arrive at the concept of sustainable competitive advantage, it is important to look at the main parts of the Resource-Based View (RBV) of the firm, starting with assets.

Assets

In the context of the Resource-Based View (RBV) of the firm, assets are considered the building blocks of a firm's resources. An asset is defined as anything that a firm owns or controls, such as physical, human, and organizational resources. Physical assets include plant and equipment, location, and access to raw materials. Human assets include the knowledge, skills, and abilities of employees, as well as their judgment, decision-making skills, and relationships. Organizational assets include the formal and informal structures, systems, and processes that enable the firm to coordinate and control its activities, as well as its culture and reputation.

Capabilities

A capability refers to the ability of a firm to perform a specific activity or task using a set of resources and assets. It is a bundle of resources that enable a firm to achieve a particular objective. Capabilities are important for a firm's success as they help in achieving its strategic objectives and gaining a competitive advantage.

A capability is usually a combination of assets and resources that are used together to perform a specific business process. For example, a firm's capability to manufacture high-quality products may involve a combination of physical assets like specialized machinery and skilled labor, as well as intangible assets like a well-defined production process, quality control systems, and employees with the necessary expertise.

Capabilities are essential for firms to achieve their strategic objectives. A firm's strategic objectives are closely linked to its capabilities, and a firm will typically focus on developing capabilities that align with its strategy. For example, a firm pursuing a differentiation strategy may focus on capabilities related to new product development, such as research and development, design, and marketing. In contrast, a firm pursuing a low-cost strategy may focus on capabilities related to process efficiency, such as lean manufacturing, supply chain optimization, and cost-cutting.

Competencies

A competency is a special capability or capacity that a firm possesses which provides it with a distinctive edge over its competitors in the market. Competencies are often a combination of resources and capabilities that are utilized together to create a unique advantage in the market.

Competencies are typically central to the firm's business model, and are often linked to the firm's core products or services. They may also be critical in enabling the firm to differentiate itself from competitors and create value for its customers. For example, Apple's competency in design and user experience has allowed them to create products that are highly differentiated and sought after by consumers. Similarly, Walmart's competency in logistics and supply chain management has enabled the company to keep costs low and compete on price.

Identifying and developing competencies is essential for a firm to maintain its competitive advantage over time. However, competencies can also become a liability if they are not maintained or adapted to changes in the market. Therefore, firms must continuously evaluate and update their competencies to remain relevant in a dynamic business environment.

Levels of Competencies

A **competence** refers to an internal capability or skill that a company possesses and performs better than its other internal capabilities. This internal capability can be a combination of resources, processes, knowledge, skills, and technologies that a firm has developed and refined over time.

A **core competence** is a specific type of competence that is central to a company's strategy, competitiveness, and profitability. It is an internal capability that is critical to the success of a company and forms the basis of its competitive advantage. Core competencies are not easily replicable by competitors and are deeply ingrained in the company's operations, culture, and people. For example, a core competence of Apple Inc. is its ability to design and develop innovative products that are aesthetically pleasing, easy to use, and seamlessly integrate hardware and software.

Finally, a **distinctive competence** refers to a specific competence that a company performs better than its competitors. It is a unique strength or advantage that sets a company apart in the marketplace. This advantage is usually based on a combination of resources, capabilities, and knowledge that are difficult for competitors to replicate. As discussed previously, Southwest Airlines has a distinctive competence in its low-cost operations model, which allows it to offer low fares while maintaining high levels of customer satisfaction and profitability.

Core competencies are critical to a company's strategy, competitiveness, and profitability, while distinctive competencies are unique strengths that set a company apart from its competitors.

A Note on Core Competencies

The concept of core competencies was introduced by C.K. Prahalad and Gary Hamel in their 1990 article "The Core Competence of the Corporation," which was later expanded upon by Prahalad and Yves Doz in their book "The Multinational Mission."

According to Prahalad and Doz, a company's core competencies are the collective learning and coordination skills that differentiate it from competitors and provide value to customers. They argue that companies should focus on developing these core competencies in order to create sustainable competitive advantage.

Prahalad and Doz suggest that there are three criteria for a core competency:

1. It must provide access to a wide variety of markets. The core competency should be applicable across different products, services, and geographic locations.

2. It should make a significant contribution to perceived customer benefits of the end product. In other words, it should provide a unique benefit to customers that is difficult for competitors to replicate.

3. It should be difficult for competitors to imitate. The core competency should be built on a complex set of skills and knowledge that is not easily acquired by competitors.

They emphasize that core competencies are not just about individual skills or resources, but rather about the integration of these resources into a cohesive whole that creates value for customers. They suggest that companies should focus on developing and leveraging their core competencies to create value for customers, rather than trying to compete on the basis of individual products or services. This focus on value creation can be the critical building block of sustainable competitive advantage.

Steps Toward SCA

Competitive advantage refers to the superiority or advantage that a company holds over its competitors in terms of factors that enable it to generate greater value for its customers and/or achieve higher profits. A competency can produce competitive advantage if it satisfies two key conditions. First, it should create value for the organization by either reducing costs or increasing revenues. For example, a company that has a core competency in efficient supply chain management can reduce its costs by sourcing materials at lower prices and delivering products to customers faster than its competitors. Second, the competency should be difficult for competitors to imitate or replicate. This can be due to a variety of factors, such as patented technology, exclusive relationships with suppliers, or specialized knowledge and expertise.

Sustainable competitive advantage is a type of competitive advantage that allows a business to maintain its advantage over a long period of time, even as competitors try to imitate or surpass it. This can be achieved through several means, such as continually innovating and improving products and services, building strong customer relationships, developing a brand identity, or creating barriers to entry in the industry through high capital requirements or regulatory restrictions. Thus, by maintaining a sustainable competitive advantage, a company can achieve long-term success and profitability.

Qualifying 'Sustainable' in SCA

When we talk about sustainable competitive advantage, the term "sustainable" refers to the ability of a firm to maintain its competitive advantage over a period of time that is sufficient enough to earn above-average profits and resist the competitive forces in the industry. It is important to note that sustainable does not mean that the advantage will last forever. It simply means that the advantage will persist for a longer period than temporary advantages, and the firm will be able to hold onto its competitive position for a sufficient amount of time.

Furthermore, sustainable does not refer to a specific length of time measured in calendar years. It depends on the industry, the rate of technological change, and other environmental factors that can impact the firm's competitive advantage. Thus, a sustainable competitive advantage suggests that a firm has a unique position in the market that is difficult for competitors to replicate, and the advantage will last long enough to make it unprofitable for competitors to try and duplicate the strategy.

VRIO: Valuable, Rare, Inimitable and Organized

VRIO is a framework used to evaluate a firm's resources and capabilities to determine their potential to contribute to a sustainable competitive advantage. The four components of VRIO are:

1. **Valuable:** The resource or capability must add value to the firm in terms of increasing revenues, reducing costs, or improving performance. If a resource or capability does not add value, it is not considered valuable.

2. **Rare:** The resource or capability must be rare or unique to the firm. If other firms in the industry have the same resource or capability, it is not considered rare.

3. **Inimitable:** The resource or capability must be difficult for competitors to imitate or replicate. If other firms can easily acquire or replicate the same resource or capability, it is not considered inimitable.

4. **Organized:** The firm must be organized to exploit the potential of the resource or capability. This includes having the necessary processes, systems, and culture in place to effectively utilize the resource or capability.

If a firm's resource or capability satisfies all four components of VRIO, it is considered to have the potential to contribute to a sustainable competitive advantage. This SCA effectively creates a barrier to entry for competitors and enables the firm to earn above-average profits. For example, Google's search algorithm is a resource that satisfies all four components of VRIO, making it a potential source of sustainable competitive advantage for the firm. The algorithm is valuable because it provides accurate and relevant search results, it is rare because no other firm has the exact same algorithm, it is inimitable because it is complex and difficult to replicate, and it is organized because Google has the necessary technology and expertise to exploit the potential of the algorithm. This satisfies all the four criteria, making it sustainable. However, this is still not a guarantee for the very long term. As we have seen recently with the introduction of ChatGPT and other AI based engines, Google may have to deal with some major threats, including to its core businesses.

What do Investors Look for?

One very common question I get from technology startups is the following: We have formed a great team to go after an exciting idea. But what do VC investors actually look for before making that first investment? This question relates to the above discussion on sustainable competitive advantage. Savvy venture investors are generally aware of the broad market trends and dynamics shaping several industries, but most often they are looking to screen startups to see if they meet certain desirable criteria, so as to provide a good chance of significant returns in the long run. They use both intuition and judgment, as well as formal analytical frameworks and techniques, before placing their bets. These generally include:

1. **Market Opportunity:** VCs want to invest in startups that are targeting large and growing markets with significant potential for revenue growth. They may use market research and analysis

to assess the size and potential of the market and evaluate the competitive landscape. VCs may look for startups that are targeting new or emerging markets, or those that are disrupting existing markets with innovative products or services. Startup teams need to demonstrate a strong understanding of their target market and have a clear plan for how to capture market share. The scalability of the startup's business model and its ability to expand into new markets may also be factors that investors will consider.

2. **Team and leadership:** VCs look for startups with experienced and talented founders and management teams who have a track record of success. They may conduct interviews and background checks to assess the team's skills, experience, and credibility. VCs want to invest in startups with leaders who have a clear vision for the future of the company and are capable of executing on that vision.

3. **Product or technology:** VCs will thoroughly assess the startup's product or technology to determine its commercial viability. They may look for evidence of product-market fit, scalability, and a competitive advantage that can be justified. Venture capitalists want to invest in startups that have innovative products or technologies that can solve real problems for customers and add value to the market.

4. **Financial performance:** VCs typically evaluate the startup's financial performance, including revenue, profitability, and cash flow. They may also evaluate the startup's financial projections

and perform sensitivity analysis to assess the potential risks and rewards of the investment. Needless to say, VCs want to invest in startups that have a clear path to profitability and can generate significant returns on their investment.

5. **Due diligence:** VCs may conduct extensive due diligence on the startup, including legal, financial, and operational due diligence. This may involve reviewing financial statements, legal agreements, customer contracts, patent filings, and other key documents, as well as conducting site visits and interviews with key stakeholders. VCs want to invest in startups that have a solid foundation and can withstand the potential risks and challenges of scaling their business.

6. **Valuation:** VCs may use a range of valuation techniques to determine the appropriate level of investment, including discounted cash flow analysis, market comparables, and precedent transactions. VCs want to invest in startups at a valuation that is reasonable and reflects the potential risks and rewards of the investment.

CHAPTER XI

Commercialization and Deployment

Commercialization and deployment are crucial steps in the creation of a new product. These are the phases at which a product is introduced to the market and made accessible for purchase by consumers. The success of a new product depends mostly on how well it does on the market. This is why commercialization and deployment are so important.

Commercialization and deployment are inextricably linked and frequently overlap. A good commercialization strategy can generate product demand, which can then drive the deployment process. A successful deployment, on the other hand, can serve to develop momentum for the product, which can aid in the commercialization process. For commercialization and deployment to go well, companies need to know a lot about the market, the product, and the competition. Since the market and competition are always changing, they must also be able to come up with new ideas and adapt to new situations. Businesses need to be ready to change their product launch strategy and product features to meet changing customer needs and stay ahead of the competition.

Constant organizational innovation is essential for commercialization and deployment success. Businesses that prioritize innovation are more likely to develop products that satisfy the market's changing needs and stay ahead of the competition. They are also more likely to design commercialization and deployment plans that are more efficient and successful. Companies that innovate can stay competitive, boost consumer satisfaction, and increase their bottom line.

Commercialization

Commercialization is the process of introducing a new product or service to the market and making it available for purchase by customers. This process has several steps, such as researching the market, designing and making the product, testing it, and making a marketing plan. The ultimate goal of commercialization is to turn a product into a profitable business venture. Hence, commercialization is a very important part of an organization's marketing function.

During the commercialization process, companies must determine how to market and sell their product or service to potential customers. This includes choosing the target market, coming up with a pricing strategy, and making a marketing campaign to get the word out about the product and get people interested in it. To make sure the product gets to the right people, the commercialization process also involves setting up sales channels and building relationships with retailers and distributors. A key aspect of commercialization is the development of a sustainable business model that can support the ongoing production and sale of the product.

This means figuring out what resources and infrastructure are needed to make and sell the product, as well as what the ongoing costs are for marketing and customer service.

Deployment

Deployment involves the actual implementation and delivery of the product or service to the end-users. To make sure the product does well on the market, it needs to be put out there in a timely and effective way.

The process of deployment typically involves several key steps, including:

1. **Launching the product:** This involves introducing the product to the market through various channels such as advertising, promotions, and social media. A successful product launch can generate buzz and interest among potential customers.

2. **Delivering the product:** This involves physically delivering the product to customers, whether through shipping, in-store pickup, or other methods. It is important to ensure that the product is delivered on time and in good condition to meet customer expectations.

3. **Training and support:** It is important to provide training and technical support to customers to ensure that they are able to use the product effectively. This can include providing user manuals, online tutorials, and other resources to help customers get started with the product.

4. **Maintenance and updates:** Products may require regular maintenance and updates to ensure that they continue to function effectively and meet customer needs. It is important to have a plan in place for addressing any issues that may arise and providing ongoing support to customers.

The success of the deployment process is closely tied to the overall success of the product in the market. Effective deployment can help to build customer loyalty and drive sales, while poor deployment can lead to customer dissatisfaction and lost sales. In order to ensure successful deployment, it is important to have a clear plan in place that addresses all of the key steps involved. This may involve working closely with marketing and sales teams to develop effective strategies, as well as collaborating with technical support teams to ensure that customers have the resources they need to use the product effectively.

Key Issues to Consider

Commercialization and deployment can be the critical drivers of marketplace success. Therefore, it is important to ensure that there is a well developed plan, along with the requisite organizational capabilities to execute on the plan, both in the short-term as the product or service is rolled out, and in the long term. Attention to the details will ensure that the launch is successful and that it stands the chance of gaining a serious competitive advantage. Some of the key issues to consider in commercialization and deployment include:

1. **Market readiness:** Before launching a new product, it is essential to ensure that the market is ready for it. This involves

conducting market research to identify the target audience, their preferences, and their willingness to pay for the product.

2. **Budget and resources:** The company must allocate adequate resources and budget for the commercialization and deployment stages. This includes funding for advertising, promotions, support infrastructure, and other expenses associated with launching the product.

3. **Competitive landscape:** The company must be aware of the competitive landscape and adjust the launch strategy and pricing accordingly. The company must differentiate its product from competitors and demonstrate its unique value proposition to potential customers.

4. **Timing:** The company must carefully choose the timing of the product launch to coincide with market trends and consumer behavior. Launching the product at the right time can significantly impact the success of the product.

5. **Scalability:** The product must be designed in a way that it can be scaled up to meet the demand in the market. The production process, supply chain, and distribution channels must be able to handle the increased volume of sales.

6. **Intellectual property:** It is essential to protect the intellectual property associated with the product through patents, trademarks, and copyrights to prevent infringement by competitors.

7. **Regulatory compliance:** The product must comply with all relevant regulations and standards. This is particularly important for products that are subject to health and safety regulations.

8. **Launch strategy:** The launch strategy must be carefully planned to generate maximum buzz and publicity for the product. This may involve advertising, promotions, and other marketing activities.

9. **Distribution channels:** The company must determine the most effective distribution channels for the product, whether it be through direct sales, retailers, or online marketplaces. It is important to ensure that the product reaches the target audience in a timely and efficient manner.

10. **Localization:** For products that will be sold in multiple markets, the company must consider localization of the product to meet the cultural and linguistic preferences of each market. This may involve adapting the product packaging, marketing materials, and support infrastructure.

11. **Support infrastructure:** The company must have a support infrastructure in place to handle customer inquiries, complaints, and technical support. This may involve setting up a customer service center or providing online support.

12. **Performance monitoring:** After the product is launched, it is important to monitor its performance in the market to identify any issues and make improvements as necessary. This may

involve collecting customer feedback, analyzing sales data, and conducting market research.

In addition to the issues outlined above, there are others that become more relevant in case existing products or technology platforms also need to be considered. These are outlined in the sections below.

Towards Continuous Innovation

In the context of commercialization and deployment, the approach to managing product life-cycles has traditionally focused on optimizing cash flow and return on investment. This often means that firms will not introduce a new generation of products while the previous one was selling well.

Consider a company producing smartphones, with its latest model selling very well in the market. Under the traditional way of thinking, the company might continue selling this model and delay introducing a new generation of smartphones until sales start to decline. However, in industries with increasing returns, this approach can be risky. For example, suppose a competitor now introduces a new generation of smartphones that offers more advanced features, better performance, and a more attractive design. Customers may switch to this new product, causing the sales of the company's previous model to decline rapidly. In this case, the company would have missed the opportunity to capture the market with a new generation of products, and it may struggle to catch up with the competitor's technological lead.

Therefore, in industries with increasing returns, it may be better for a company to invest in continuous innovation and introduce new generations of products regularly, even if the previous generation is selling well. In effect, the sales of the previous generation of products is being cannibalized by the new release, and it is being done so willingly. By doing so, the company can make it difficult for competitors to gain a technological lead and maintain its market position.

As pointed out previously in a section discussing organizational culture, it is vital that companies create and inculcate an environment that fosters innovation and creativity. Some quick methods to build these capabilities in organizations include:

1. **Encourage risk-taking:** Encourage employees to take risks and pursue new ideas without fear of failure. Provide a safe space for experimentation and learning from mistakes.

2. **Foster a culture of creativity:** Encourage creativity by providing opportunities for employees to brainstorm, collaborate, and share ideas. Provide resources for training and development in creative problem-solving techniques.

3. **Invest in R&D:** Allocate resources for research and development activities that support innovation. Invest in new technologies, equipment, and software that enable innovation.

4. **Implement an innovation process:** Implement a structured innovation process that involves ideation, selection, development, testing, and implementation. This process should be transparent and accessible to all employees.

5. **Reward innovation:** Create a system of rewards and recognition that encourages and incentivizes innovation. This can include monetary rewards, promotions, or other forms of recognition.

6. **Partner with external stakeholders:** Partner with external stakeholders such as customers, suppliers, and academic institutions to gain access to new ideas, technologies, and perspectives.

7. **Develop a diverse workforce:** Create a diverse and inclusive workforce that brings a variety of perspectives and experiences to the innovation process. This can include hiring employees from different backgrounds and cultures, as well as promoting diversity and inclusion in the workplace.

Compatible or Not?

A similar balancing act occurs when a firm considers how its product should relate to both earlier generations of its products, as well as complementary products in the marketplace. Thus a decision needs to be made on whether or not a product needs to be protected, and to what extent. Protecting it too little can lead to the development of low-quality copies and similar products by competitors, while protecting it too much can stifle innovation and the development of complementary products. Therefore, companies must carefully decide on how compatible their products will be with those of others and whether to make them backward compatible with previous generations.

Typically, if a company is dominant in the market, it usually prefers incompatibility with others' platforms (e.g. Apple), but may use controlled licensing for complements. On the other hand, if a company is at an installed base disadvantage, it generally prefers some compatibility with others and aggressive licensing to complements to attract customers (e.g. Linux).

In the case where both the installed base and complements are crucial, backward compatibility is usually the best approach as it leverages the installed base and complements of the previous generation and links generations together. This approach can also be combined with incentives to upgrade to the latest version of the product.

CHAPTER XII

Other Strategy Concepts

In addition to the previous themes and concepts we have explored so far, there are many others derived from the field of business strategy that can be applied to any analysis where technology plays a role. Given their generality and range of applicability, we have grouped them together in this section. Depending on the context and the problem you are trying to solve, you can selectively apply these concepts, frameworks and tools.

Strategic Planning

Strategic planning is the process of defining an organization's strategy or direction and making decisions on allocating its resources to pursue this strategy. It involves setting goals, analyzing internal and external factors, and creating action plans to achieve those goals.

In the context of a technology company, strategic planning involves understanding the technology landscape, identifying potential opportunities and threats, and leveraging technology to achieve business objectives. This process may involve assessing the company's strengths and weaknesses, analyzing market trends and competitors, identifying customer needs, and creating a roadmap for innovation and growth.

Technology companies may also need to consider factors such as intellectual property protection, regulatory compliance, and talent acquisition and retention as part of their strategic planning process. Effective strategic planning can help technology companies stay ahead of the curve and remain competitive in a rapidly changing industry.

Technology Roadmapping

Roadmapping is a strategic planning method used to align a company's goals with its actions and investments over time. It involves visualizing and planning out the various stages of a project or product development, including milestones and key performance indicators (KPIs), to ensure that the company is on track to achieve its objectives. Roadmapping is particularly useful for companies that operate in rapidly changing industries or markets, as it allows them to adapt and pivot their strategies as needed. By providing a clear roadmap, the company can also communicate its plans and progress to stakeholders and investors.

A technology roadmap is a strategic plan that outlines the development and implementation of new technologies within an organization. It can be used to identify and prioritize research and development projects, allocate resources, and plan for future investments in technology. It can help organizations stay competitive by keeping up with industry trends and advancements, and ensuring that their technology infrastructure is up-to-date and efficient. Additionally, it can facilitate communication and collaboration among different departments within the organization.

Samsung, for example, begins its technology roadmapping process with a thorough analysis of the industry landscape, taking into account consumer preferences and competitive offerings. The company then conducts an internal assessment of its technology capabilities, including research and development initiatives and intellectual property portfolios. This helps Samsung identify any gaps in its technology and ensure that it has the necessary resources to bring new products to market. Based on this analysis, Samsung develops a roadmap that outlines specific milestones and targets for future product releases. The roadmap could include key performance indicators, such as battery life, processing speed, and camera quality, for example, and also identifies potential technological advancements that could help Samsung differentiate its products from competitors.

The table below shows a sample breakdown of the elements of a sample technology roadmap:

Key Element	Example
Visioning	Provide affordable and accessible water purification globally
Technology Assessment	Evaluation of current water purification methods, emerging technologies, competitive landscape
Market Analysis	Understanding water scarcity challenges, customer needs, pricing, partnerships
Resource Assessment	Audit of internal skills, expertise, facilities, budget, personnel
Roadmapping	Chart showing evolution of water purification products/services over 5/10/15 year horizons
Implementation Planning	Specific schedules, budgets, milestones to execute roadmap deliverables
Marketing and Evaluation	Go-to-market strategy, positioning, customer feedback, iteration

Table: Breakdown of a Sample Technology Roadmap

A product roadmap, on the other hand, is a strategic plan that outlines the development and launch of a specific product or product line. It includes details such as target market, product features, development timeline, and expected launch date.

Roadmapping is useful because it helps companies stay focused on their long-term goals, prioritize investments, and ensure that their resources are being allocated effectively. It also enables companies to anticipate and plan for potential challenges or obstacles along the way, and to adjust their plans accordingly. Additionally, roadmapping can help companies communicate their plans and progress to stakeholders both within and outside the organization.

Benchmarking

Benchmarking is a process by which a firm compares its own performance, processes, or strategies to those of other firms considered to be industry leaders or best-in-class. It is used to identify areas of improvement, set performance targets, and develop action plans to enhance the firm's competitiveness.

In technology strategy, benchmarking can be used to assess a firm's performance in areas such as product development, research and development, innovation, and technology adoption. By comparing its own practices with those of other industry players, a firm can identify areas where it is falling behind and develop strategies to catch up or exceed the competition. For example, a software development company may benchmark its product development cycle against that of a leading competitor to identify ways to improve time-to-market and innovation. Additionally, benchmarking can be used to identify best practices in areas such as technology adoption, such as implementing agile methodologies or using artificial intelligence in operations. Overall, benchmarking is a useful tool in technology strategy as it helps firms identify areas for improvement and stay competitive in a rapidly evolving industry. Benchmarking can also provide valuable insights into customer preferences and expectations, allowing firms to tailor their products and services to better meet the needs of their target market. By understanding what customers value most, companies can gain a competitive advantage and improve customer satisfaction. In summary, benchmarking is an essential practice for any technology firm looking to stay ahead of the competition and meet the evolving needs of its customers.

CHAPTER XIII

Technology Forecasting

Importance of Forecasts

In order to better understand emerging technology areas, it is important to be aware of some of the common tools that can be used for forecasting. In the sections below, we will cover some of the major types of tools that can be useful.

Forecasting the future is a critical aspect of strategic planning for businesses and organizations. Accurate forecasts can provide insights into the future trends and changes, enabling businesses to plan ahead and adapt to the changing market conditions. In this section, we will discuss various forecasting techniques that can help organizations view the future looking out 5 to 10 years.

Forecasting Techniques

Forecasting techniques can be broadly classified into two categories: qualitative and quantitative. Qualitative methods rely on subjective judgment, opinions, and expert knowledge to predict future trends, while quantitative methods use statistical models to analyze historical data and predict future trends. The choice of forecasting technique depends on the nature of the problem, the data availability, and the level of accuracy required.

Trend Extrapolations

Trend extrapolations are the simplest and most common forecasting technique. Trend extrapolation is a forecasting technique that assumes the future will be a continuation of the past. Thus, this technique is based on the idea that historical data can be used to identify patterns and trends that will continue into the future. Trend extrapolation can be used for both short-term and long-term forecasting.

The first step in trend extrapolation is to identify the historical data that is relevant to the forecast. This data can include sales figures, market trends, and economic indicators. The next step is to use statistical methods to identify the trend in the data. Once the trend has been identified, it can be extrapolated into the future to make a forecast.

Trend extrapolation is a simple and straightforward forecasting technique that can be used to make short-term and long-term forecasts. However, it is important to note that trend extrapolation assumes that the future will be a continuation of the past. This may not always be the case, especially in industries that are subject to disruptive innovations.

Expert Consensus

Expert consensus is a qualitative forecasting technique that relies on the opinions and judgment of experts in the field. This technique is based on the idea that experts in a particular field have a better understanding of the trends and developments that are likely to occur in the future.

To use expert consensus for forecasting, a panel of experts is first selected in the relevant field (for example. a group of surgeons or medical specialists giving their inputs on). The experts are then asked to provide their opinions on the future trends and developments in the field. The opinions are then aggregated to provide a forecast of the future. Expert consensus can be a useful technique when there is a high degree of uncertainty about the future. By relying on the opinions of experts, it is possible to get a more accurate picture of the future than by relying on statistical methods alone. However, it is important to note that expert consensus can be biased by the opinions and perspectives of the experts themselves.

The Delphi method is a commonly used form of expert consensus, and consists of a structured process for collecting and distilling knowledge from a panel of experts through a series of rounds of questionnaires and feedback. In this method, a group of experts are asked to provide their individual opinions and judgments on a particular topic or question, and then their responses are analyzed and summarized by a facilitator, who then feeds back the results to the group. The experts are then asked to revise and refine their responses in light of the feedback and the responses of their peers. This process is repeated until a consensus is reached or until the facilitator determines that further rounds are not necessary. The Delphi method is particularly useful in situations where there is a lack of reliable data or when the issue at hand is complex and multifaceted. It allows for the integration of diverse perspectives and can result in more accurate and informed decision-making.

Simulation Methods

Simulation methods are forecasting techniques that use computer models to simulate the behavior of complex systems in order to predict future outcomes. Simulation methods are often used in industries such as aerospace, defense, and finance, where complex systems are common.

To use simulation methods for forecasting, a computer model is first created that simulates the behavior of the system (i.e. the system is modeled). The model is then run with different inputs to see how the system responds. The results of the simulation can then be used to make a forecast of the future.

Simulation methods can be useful for forecasting when there are complex systems involved that are difficult to model using traditional forecasting techniques. However, simulation methods can be expensive and time-consuming to develop and run. They also require a significant amount of data to accurately predict future outcomes, and the accuracy of the forecast is highly dependent on the quality of the input data used in the simulation.

Scenario Planning

Scenario planning is a forecasting technique that involves creating different scenarios of the future based on different assumptions and factors. It is based on the idea that there are multiple possible futures, and that it is important to consider different scenarios to make informed decisions about the future.

To use scenario planning for forecasting, different scenarios are created based on different assumptions and factors. These scenarios are then analyzed to see how they might affect the future. The results of the analysis can then be used to make a forecast of the future.

This technique can be useful for forecasting when there is a high degree of uncertainty about the future. By considering different scenarios, it is possible to identify potential risks and opportunities that may not be apparent. We cover scenario planning in more detail in Chapter XIV. Tools and Frameworks.

Decision Trees

Decision trees are a quantitative forecasting technique that involves mapping out different decision paths and outcomes. Decision trees are useful when there are multiple options and outcomes and the decision-making process is complex. Decision trees can be used to analyze the trade-offs between different options and provide insights into the likely outcomes.

Decision trees are often used in industries such as finance, healthcare, and marketing. For example, a financial institution may use a decision tree to determine whether to approve or reject a loan application. The decision tree would map out the various factors that influence the decision, such as the applicant's credit score, income, and employment history. The tree would then provide different outcomes based on the decision, such as approving the loan, denying the loan, or requesting more information. Usually, these decision trees are built on large datasets in order to ensure reasonable accuracy and fairness.

Decision trees can be a powerful tool for analyzing complex decision-making processes and providing insights into likely outcomes. However, they require careful planning and analysis to ensure that the tree accurately reflects the decision-making process and provides reliable insights.

Hybrid Methods

Hybrid methods involve combining different forecasting techniques to improve the accuracy and reliability of the forecast. For example, a hybrid method may combine trend extrapolation with expert consensus to improve the accuracy of the forecast. Hybrid methods often combine quantitative and qualitative forecasting techniques. For example, a hybrid method may combine trend extrapolation with expert opinion to gain a better understanding of the future trends and changes. This approach allows organizations to integrate data-driven and subjective insights into their forecasting process. Hybrid methods are useful when the data is complex, and the future is uncertain.

Predicting the future is challenging, and no forecasting technique is perfect. However, by using a combination of different techniques and approaches, organizations can gain a better understanding of the future trends and changes and plan ahead. The use of hybrid methods can help organizations to reduce potential errors and biases in their forecasting process, given that they provide a more comprehensive and balanced view of the future. This can lead to better decision-making and improved business outcomes.

Emerging Areas

The field of technology strategy is very broad and will continue to have major implications for how firms are created, evolve, and grow in the future. There are significant advances in several scientific and technological areas that are driving the need for skilled professionals who can bring their knowledge of technology strategy, combined with the tools and frameworks for analysis. Some of the exciting domains which you should consider for an opportunity to apply your knowledge and skills in this topic include:

1. **Digital transformation:** This topic involves the use of technology to fundamentally change business models and operations. It includes the adoption of new technologies such as artificial intelligence, machine learning, and big data analytics to improve efficiency and customer experience.

2. **Platform business models:** Platforms such as Uber, Airbnb, and Amazon have disrupted traditional industries and created new markets. This topic explores the strategies that companies use to build and scale platform businesses.

3. **Internet of Things (IoT):** The IoT involves the interconnectivity of devices, sensors, and machines to collect and share data. This technology has the potential to transform industries such as healthcare, manufacturing, and transportation.

4. **Genomics:** The study of the human genome has led to new opportunities for personalized medicine and drug development. This topic explores the business strategies and challenges associated with genomics research and development.

5. **Omics:** Omics refers to the study of biological molecules such as genes, proteins, and metabolites. This field has the potential to

transform healthcare by enabling personalized medicine and improving disease diagnosis and treatment. Omics also presents challenges related to data management, privacy, and ethics.

6. **Artificial intelligence (AI):** AI is being used to develop intelligent systems that can perform complex tasks and make decisions without human intervention. AI has the potential to transform industries such as healthcare, finance, and manufacturing. The speed of advancements in AI presents major challenges and opens up new opportunities for all sectors of the economy.

7. **Quantum computing:** Quantum computing is a rapidly growing area of technology that promises to revolutionize the way we process information. The basic principle of quantum computing is to use quantum bits or qubits, which can exist in multiple states simultaneously, allowing for exponentially more complex computations than classical computing. This makes quantum computing ideal for solving complex problems that are beyond the capabilities of classical computers. One of the most promising applications of quantum computing is in the field of cryptography, where it has the potential to provide unparalleled security. Quantum computers can use the principles of quantum mechanics to crack complex mathematical problems that are used to encrypt data. This means that quantum computers could be used to crack many of the encryption methods that are currently used to protect sensitive data, such as financial transactions and government communications.

8. **Blockchain Technologies:** Blockchain is a distributed database or ledger that enables secure, tamper-proof transactions without the need for intermediaries such as banks or governments. It is built on a network of computers that verify and store each transaction, making it virtually impossible to alter or hack. This technology was first developed in 2008 as the underlying technology for Bitcoin, a digital currency, but has since evolved to have much broader applications beyond just finance. One of the main benefits of blockchain technology is that it allows for secure and transparent transactions between parties without the need for a trusted intermediary. This can lead to cost savings and increased efficiency in industries such as supply chain management and logistics, where tracking goods and verifying their authenticity is essential. In healthcare, blockchain can be used to securely store and share patient data, enabling better collaboration between healthcare providers and reducing the risk of data breaches. Another key feature of blockchain is its ability to create smart contracts, which are self-executing contracts with the terms of the agreement between buyer and seller being directly written into lines of code. These contracts can be used to automate business processes and reduce the need for intermediaries, further increasing efficiency and reducing costs.

9. **Cybersecurity:** With the growing threat of cyberattacks, cybersecurity has become a critical topic for businesses. This topic explores the strategies that companies use to protect their systems and data from cyber threats.

10. **Sustainability and Green Technology:** Companies are increasingly focusing on sustainability and using technology to reduce their environmental impact. This includes using renewable energy sources, reducing waste, and developing more efficient products and services.

11. **Cloud Computing:** Cloud computing is becoming the de facto standard for storing and accessing data and applications. Companies are using cloud computing to reduce costs, increase agility, and improve scalability.

12. **Open Innovation:** Open innovation refers to the practice of collaborating with external partners such as customers, suppliers, and startups to generate new ideas and accelerate innovation.

13. **E-Commerce and Omnichannel Retail:** E-commerce and omnichannel retail are transforming how businesses sell products and services. Companies must develop strategies to compete in an increasingly crowded and competitive online marketplace.

CHAPTER XIV

Tools and Frameworks

The Five Forces Model

The Five Forces model is a framework for analyzing the competitive forces that shape an industry's structure and profitability. First proposed by Prof. Michael Porter of Harvard Business School, it is also popularly known as Porter's Five Forces Model. It includes five key forces: the threat of new entrants, the bargaining power of suppliers, the bargaining power of buyers, the threat of substitute products or services, and the intensity of competitive rivalry. By assessing the strength of each of these forces, organizations can determine their competitive position within the industry and develop strategies to improve it.

In technology strategy, Porter's Five Forces model is an important tool because it helps organizations understand the competitive dynamics of the industry in which they operate. This allows them to identify areas where they can differentiate themselves from competitors and improve their competitive position. For example, by assessing the threat of new entrants, an organization can determine if there are high barriers to entry that can prevent new competitors from entering the market. By understanding the bargaining power of suppliers and buyers, organizations can negotiate better deals and improve their profitability. Ultimately, using Porter's Five Forces model as part of a technology strategy can help organizations make informed decisions about where to focus their resources and how to compete effectively in their industry.

The key takeaways from Porter's Five Forces model are as follows:

1. **Threat of new entrants:** New entrants increase competition and lower profits. Barriers to entry can include economies of scale, brand recognition, and government regulations.

2. **Bargaining power of suppliers:** Suppliers with significant bargaining power can demand higher prices and better terms, reducing profitability. Supplier power can be influenced by factors such as switching costs and the availability of substitutes.

3. **Bargaining power of buyers:** Buyers with significant bargaining power can demand lower prices and better terms, also reducing profitability. Buyer power can be influenced by factors such as the availability of substitutes and the importance of the product to the buyer.

4. **Threat of substitutes:** The availability of substitutes can reduce demand and profitability. Substitutes can include products or services from other industries or alternative technologies.

5. **Rivalry among existing competitors:** Intense competition among existing competitors can lead to price wars and reduced profits. Industry rivalry can be influenced by factors such as the number of competitors, industry growth, and product differentiation.

We can use Porter's Five Forces to analyze any industry. Consider the hardware industry and the market for personal computers (PCs). The threat of new entrants is relatively low in this industry due to high barriers to entry such as economies of scale and brand recognition. The bargaining power of suppliers is moderate due to the availability of multiple suppliers and the ability of PC manufacturers to switch suppliers. The bargaining power of buyers is high due to the availability of substitutes and the importance of price to consumers. The threat of substitutes is high due to the availability of smartphones and tablets. Rivalry among existing competitors is intense due to the large number of PC manufacturers and the similarity of their products. Overall, we can observe that the PC industry is characterized by high competition and low profitability.

How to Use the Five Forces Model?

Here are some simple steps for using Porter's Five Forces Model while formulating an overall strategy. You can typically also provide such an analysis in a business plan or roadmap:

1. **Identify the five forces:** The five forces in Porter's model are the threat of new entrants, the bargaining power of suppliers, the bargaining power of buyers, the threat of substitute products or services, and the intensity of competitive rivalry. Identify each of these forces for your industry.

2. **Assess the strength of each force:** For each force, assess how strong it is in your industry. As an example we discussed earlier, in the hardware industry, the bargaining power of suppliers might be strong because there are only a few suppliers of key components.

3. **Determine the overall attractiveness of the industry:** Based on the strength of each force, determine the overall attractiveness of the industry. A more attractive industry will have weaker forces, while a less attractive industry will have stronger forces.

4. **Develop a strategy:** Based on your analysis of the industry, develop a strategy for your company. For example, if the threat of new entrants is low, you may want to focus on expanding your market share. If the bargaining power of buyers is high, you may want to focus on differentiation to make your product more attractive.

The table below provides a list of the five forces, along with the key questions you should be asking while considering their impact. If you can answer a majority of these questions based on analysis of real data, you will have a much better grasp of the industry dynamics than when you first started the analysis.

Force	Key Questions to Ask
Competitive Rivalry	Who are the major competitors? What is the industry growth rate? How differentiated are competitor offerings? What are the switching costs? How intense is the battle for market share?
Supplier Power	How concentrated are suppliers? Are there substitute inputs? Are suppliers integrated with buyers? Do suppliers pose a threat of forward integration? How much does quality or service vary between suppliers? How easy is it to switch suppliers?
Buyer Power	How concentrated or informed are buyers? How easy is it for buyers to switch suppliers? Are buyers a threat for backward integration? Do buyers purchase large volumes? How price sensitive are buyers?
Threat of Substitutes	Are there close substitute products? Do substitutes offer an attractive price-performance tradeoff? What are the switching costs to substitutes? What is the propensity for customers to substitute?
Threat of New Entrants	What are the entry barriers (capital, regulation, economies of scale)? How likely is retaliation from incumbents? Are there proprietary advantages or privileged access to raw materials/distribution?

Table: Applying The Five Forces Model

Overall, Porter's Five Forces Model can be a valuable tool for understanding the competitive dynamics of an industry and making informed strategic decisions.

The Strategy Diamond

The Strategy Diamond is a framework that was developed by Donald Hambrick and James Frederickson in their book "Are You Sure You Have a Strategy?" It is a tool that helps organizations assess and align various elements of their strategy, including arenas, differentiators, vehicles, staging and pacing, and economic logic. A brief description of each element of the Strategy Diamond follows:

1. **Arenas:** The arenas or markets in which the organization chooses to compete. This includes specific geographies, customer segments, and product categories.

2. **Differentiators:** The key factors that set the organization apart from its competitors. This can include unique product features, customer service, marketing, and branding.

3. **Vehicles:** The specific channels or ways in which the organization will reach its target customers. This can include direct sales, online sales, partnerships, and distribution networks.

4. **Staging and Pacing:** The organization's approach to timing and sequencing its actions. This includes deciding when to enter or exit markets, launch new products, or scale up or down operations.

5. **Economic Logic:** The organization's approach to creating value and generating profit. This includes pricing strategies, cost management, and revenue models.

The Strategy Diamond is useful for analysis as it allows organizations to consider all of these elements together and assess how well they align with each other. For example, an organization may have a great product differentiator, but if it is entering the wrong arenas or using ineffective vehicles, it may not achieve success. The framework can also help organizations identify areas of weakness and potential areas for improvement in their strategy.

Technology Assessment Model (TAM)

The Technology Assessment Model (TAM) is a tool used to evaluate the potential benefits and risks associated with new technologies. The model was developed by the National Institute of Standards and Technology (NIST) in the United States and is designed to help organizations assess the value of a new technology before making a significant investment.

The TAM framework consists of four main steps:

1. **Identify the technology and its applications:** This involves understanding the basic functions and capabilities of the technology and how it could potentially be used in the organization.

2. **Determine the benefits and risks:** This step involves identifying the potential benefits of the technology, such as improved efficiency, cost savings, or new product offerings, as well as the potential risks, such as security vulnerabilities, privacy concerns, or regulatory compliance issues.

3. **Evaluate the technology:** In this step, the organization evaluates the technology against a set of criteria, such as technical feasibility, scalability, or compatibility with existing systems.

4. **Make a decision:** Based on the results of the evaluation, the organization can make an informed decision about whether to invest in the technology or not.

The TAM model is often used by government agencies and large corporations to evaluate the potential impact of emerging technologies, such as artificial intelligence, blockchain, or Internet of Things (IoT). The key takeaway from TAM is the importance of assessing both the benefits and risks of a new technology before making a significant investment to ensure that the organization is making informed decisions based on a thorough evaluation.

Technology Acceptance Model (TAM)

The Technology Acceptance Model (TAM) is a theoretical framework that explains how users accept and adopt new technologies. It was first introduced by Fred Davis in 1989 and has been widely used in research to study technology adoption behavior.

The model is based on two main constructs: perceived usefulness and perceived ease of use. Perceived usefulness refers to the user's belief that a technology will enhance their job performance or make their life easier. Perceived ease of use refers to the user's belief that a technology is easy to use and learn.

According to the TAM, perceived usefulness and ease of use are the key determinants of a user's intention to use a new technology. If a user perceives a technology to be useful and easy to use, they are more likely to adopt it.

We can summarize the key takeaways from the Technology Acceptance Model (TAM) as follows:

1. **Perceived usefulness:** A technology is more likely to be adopted if users perceive it as useful and valuable.

2. **Perceived ease of use:** The ease of use of a technology is another critical factor in its adoption. Users are more likely to adopt a technology that is easy to use.

3. **Attitude towards use:** Users' attitude towards using a technology plays a significant role in its adoption. Positive attitudes increase the likelihood of adoption.

4. **Behavioral intention to use:** Users' intention to use a technology predicts their actual use. If users have a positive intention to use a technology, they are more likely to adopt and use it.

5. **Actual system use:** The actual use of a technology is the final outcome of the adoption process. It is influenced by the previous four factors and other external factors.

6. **Social influence:** The influence of social factors, such as the opinions of peers and colleagues, can affect users' perceptions of a technology and their intention to use it.

7. **Perceived credibility:** The credibility of the technology and the source of information about the technology can also affect users' perceptions and adoption decisions.

The TAM has been used in a variety of settings, including healthcare, education, and business, to study technology adoption behavior. This model has also been widely used to explain and predict user acceptance of popular technologies like mobile apps, social media platforms, and online shopping websites. TAM has proven itself to be a useful framework for predicting user behavior and identifying factors that may affect technology adoption. We can therefore conclude that TAM can be used by organizations to design and implement technology systems that are more likely to be adopted and effectively used by their intended users.

Modified Technology Acceptance Model (MTAM)

The Modified Technology Acceptance Model (MTAM) is a framework for assessing the potential success of new technologies within an organization. It is based on the Technology Acceptance Model (TAM), but expands on it by taking into account organizational and environmental factors that can affect technology adoption.

While TAM focuses primarily on individual-level factors that influence technology acceptance, such as perceived usefulness and ease of use, MTAM takes a broader view by also considering factors such as top management support, compatibility with existing systems, and regulatory issues.

In MTAM, technology acceptance is viewed as a multi-level process, with individual-level factors being nested within organizational-level and environmental-level factors. By taking into account these broader factors, MTAM provides a more comprehensive picture of the factors that can influence technology adoption within an organization.

Overall, MTAM offers a more nuanced and detailed approach to technology assessment compared to TAM. It recognizes that technology adoption is a complex process that is influenced by a wide range of factors, and provides a framework for considering these factors in a systematic way.

Case Examples: TAM and MTAM

TAM: Consider a study of consumer adoption of mobile banking. A researcher could use the TAM to understand the factors that influence a consumer's decision to adopt mobile banking. The researcher would measure the perceived usefulness and perceived ease of use of mobile banking, as well as other factors like the consumer's attitudes towards technology, their trust in the banking institution, and their previous experience with mobile banking.

MTAM: Consider a study of healthcare professionals' adoption of electronic health records (EHRs). A researcher could use the MTAM to understand the factors that influence a healthcare professional's decision to adopt EHRs. The researcher would measure the perceived usefulness and perceived ease of use of EHRs, as well as other factors like the professional's attitudes towards technology, their perceived compatibility with their work practices, and their social influence from colleagues and patients. The MTAM expands on the TAM by including additional factors like compatibility and social influence that are particularly relevant in healthcare settings.

Blue Ocean Strategy

The Blue Ocean Strategy is a business strategy that involves creating a new, uncontested market space that makes competitors irrelevant. It was introduced by W. Chan Kim and Renée Mauborgne in their 2005 book, "Blue Ocean Strategy."

The strategy encourages firms to shift their focus from competing in an existing market space (a "red ocean" where many competitors fight for the same customers) to creating a new market space (a "blue ocean" where no competition exists). This can be done by identifying and meeting previously unmet customer needs or by creating entirely new customer groups.

The Blue Ocean Strategy can be applied to both new and existing firms. For new firms, it can be used to identify a unique business idea that can compete effectively in the market. For existing firms, it can be used to rejuvenate a stagnant business by identifying new growth opportunities and creating new market space.

The key takeaways from the Blue Ocean Strategy are:

1. Focus on creating new demand rather than fighting for existing demand.

2. Identify and meet previously unmet customer needs.

3. Create new market space by offering a unique value proposition.

4. Avoid head-to-head competition and focus on differentiation.

5. Constantly innovate and adapt to changing market conditions.

By following the Blue Ocean Strategy, firms can differentiate themselves from their competitors, create new market space, and achieve sustained growth and profitability.

The S-Curve

S-curves are a graphical representation of the growth or adoption of a new technology or innovation over time. The curve takes its name from its shape, which resembles the letter "S" when plotted on a graph. The S-curve typically starts slowly as the new technology is introduced and begins to gain traction, then experiences rapid growth as adoption accelerates, and eventually slows down as the technology reaches its limits of adoption or matures.

S-curves are important in technology and innovation because they provide a way to visualize and understand the pattern of adoption and growth of a new technology. By analyzing the S-curve, researchers and managers can gain insights into the factors that influence the adoption and diffusion of the technology, as well as the timing and rate of growth. This understanding can be used to develop effective strategies for introducing and promoting the technology, as well as to anticipate and manage the eventual decline in adoption and growth.

One inference that can be drawn from the S-curve is the expected lifespan of the technology. The curve typically reaches its maximum growth rate when the technology has achieved a critical mass of adoption and usage. Once this point is reached, the technology may begin to plateau and eventually decline as it becomes obsolete or is replaced by newer technologies. Another inference that can be drawn from the S-curve is the expected rate of adoption. The shape of the curve can provide insight into the speed at which the technology is likely to be adopted by different groups of users, as well as the potential barriers to adoption that may need to be overcome.

The Hype Cycle

The hype cycle is a graphical representation developed by Gartner, a leading research and advisory company, that illustrates the adoption and diffusion of new technologies. It consists of five stages that a new technology typically goes through before it becomes mainstream.

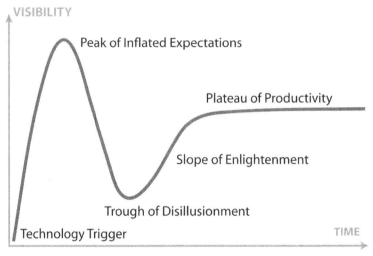

Fig. The Hype Cycle
(Source: Gartner Research)

1. **Technology Trigger:** The first stage is the introduction of a new technology. At this stage, there is a lot of excitement and buzz around the potential of the technology. The technology is not yet fully developed and has not been tested in the market.

2. **Peak of Inflated Expectations:** In this stage, the hype around the technology reaches its peak. Everyone is talking about it, and there is a lot of excitement and optimism. However, there is often little evidence to support the hype, and the technology has not yet been widely adopted.

3. **Trough of Disillusionment:** At this stage, the hype dies down, and the reality of the technology sets in. People realize that the technology is not as revolutionary as they initially thought, and

174

adoption rates are slow. Many companies and individuals abandon the technology altogether.

4. **Slope of Enlightenment:** In this stage, the technology begins to mature, and its true value becomes apparent. Companies and individuals start to find innovative ways to use the technology, and adoption rates begin to rise again.

5. **Plateau of Productivity:** The final stage is when the technology becomes mainstream and widely adopted. The technology is fully integrated into people's lives and businesses, and its value is widely recognized.

The hype cycle is important in that it provides a unique framework for understanding the adoption and diffusion of new technologies, especially those which are subjected to constant attention and coverage. By understanding where a technology is in the hype cycle, businesses and individuals can make informed decisions about whether to invest in the technology, how to market the technology, and when to expect widespread adoption. The hype cycle also highlights the importance of managing expectations and understanding the potential risks and challenges associated with new technologies.

One example of a technology that followed the hype cycle is virtual reality (VR). In the 1990s, VR was hyped as the future of entertainment, education, and even communication. However, the technology was not yet mature enough to deliver on these promises, and interest in VR waned. In the mid-2010s, advances in VR technology reignited interest in the technology, and it began to climb the "Peak of Inflated

Expectations" on the hype cycle. Companies like Oculus, HTC, and Sony invested heavily in VR, and many predicted that VR would soon become mainstream. However, the technology struggled to deliver on these expectations, and entered the "Trough of Disillusionment." Consumers complained about issues like motion sickness, high cost, and limited content, and interest in VR waned again. Today, VR is still in the process of climbing the "Slope of Enlightenment." While it has not yet achieved mainstream adoption, VR is finding niche applications in areas like gaming, healthcare, and education, and many experts believe that it has significant potential for the future.

Evaluating New Technologies

There are several common frameworks used to evaluate new technologies. Here are a few examples:

1. **Technology Readiness Level (TRL):** This framework is used to assess the maturity level of a technology. The TRL scale ranges from 1 to 9, with 1 being the lowest level of maturity (basic principles observed) and 9 being the highest (technology proven in actual use).

2. **Technology Scouting:** This framework involves the identification, analysis, and selection of new technologies that can provide competitive advantage. Technology scouting involves a combination of market and technology research, and often involves collaboration with external partners such as universities and research institutions.

3. **SWOT Analysis:** This framework is a commonly used tool for evaluating the strengths, weaknesses, opportunities, and threats associated with a new technology. SWOT analysis can be used to identify potential risks and opportunities associated with a technology, as well as to assess its potential impact on existing products and services.

4. **Cost-Benefit Analysis:** This framework involves the assessment of the costs and benefits associated with a new technology. This analysis can help to determine whether a technology is financially viable, and can also provide insight into the potential economic and societal impact of the technology.

5. **Business Model Canvas:** This framework is a visual tool used to describe, analyze, and design a new technology business model. It includes nine building blocks that cover all aspects of a business, including customer segments, value propositions, revenue streams, and cost structure. The canvas can help to identify key challenges and opportunities associated with a new technology, and can be used to develop a comprehensive business plan.

Overall, these frameworks can provide a structured approach to evaluating new technologies and can help to identify key opportunities and challenges associated with their development and commercialization. We take a more detailed look at the Business Model Canvas next.

SCRUM and Agile Development

SCRUM and agile development are project management approaches that have become increasingly popular in recent years. These techniques, which are built on the ideas of flexibility, cooperation, and rapid iteration, have proven to be extremely effective in the management of complex technology projects. SCRUM was first described by Jeff Sutherland and Ken Schwaber in 1995, in a paper titled "SCRUM Development Process." The term "SCRUM" itself was borrowed from rugby, where it refers to a group of players who work together to move the ball down the field. The authors developed the SCRUM methodology based on their experiences managing software development projects, and they have continued to refine and develop it over the years. Agile development, on the other hand, is a broader methodology that encompasses a range of different approaches, including SCRUM. The Agile Manifesto, a document that outlines the key principles of Agile development, was developed in 2001 by a group of software developers, including Kent Beck, Ward Cunningham, and Martin Fowler. The Agile Manifesto emphasizes flexibility, collaboration, and rapid iteration, and it has become a widely adopted approach to managing software development projects.

Element	Description	Example
Product Backlog	Prioritized list of desired product features and requirements	List of required features for a new app release
Sprints	Fixed duration cycles to deliver increments of work	2 week sprints to add new features
Sprint Planning	Plan user stories to be completed in the sprint	Team meets to select stories for upcoming sprint
Daily Standups	Short daily sync on progress and obstacles	15 minute standup meeting to report status
Sprint Review	Review and demonstrate completed stories	Demo new features to stakeholders after sprint
Sprint Retrospective	Reflect on efficiency of last sprint and identify improvements	Discuss ways to improve collaboration for next sprint
Ship Increment	Working software system from completed sprints	Release new version of app after milestone

Table: Applying SCRUM

One of the most significant advantages of SCRUM and Agile development is that they enable firms to adjust quickly to changing market conditions and consumer needs. They make it easy to modify priorities and pivot when necessary by dividing projects down into smaller, more manageable tasks. As a result, these techniques are particularly pertinent to technology strategy, where the ability to adjust quickly to changing technological and market situations is critical.

These methodologies encourage team members to collaborate and communicate with one another, thus encouraging a culture of innovation and continuous development by emphasizing regular check-ins, feedback, and cooperation. Customer satisfaction is also emphasized, with a focus on ensuring that organizations offer products and services that fulfill the needs of their target market by incorporating clients in the development process. These approaches have proven to be highly effective in managing complex technology projects and delivering successful technology strategies by allowing firms to adjust quickly to changing market conditions, increasing collaboration and communication, and stressing customer satisfaction.

Business Model Canvas

The Business Model Canvas (BMC) is a strategic management tool that provides a visual representation of a business model. It was created by Alexander Osterwalder and Yves Pigneur and first published in their book "Business Model Generation" in 2010.

The BMC consists of nine key components, which are:

1. **Customer Segments:** The specific groups of customers that a business is targeting.

2. **Value Proposition:** The products or services that a business is offering to its customers and the unique value it provides to them.

3. **Channels:** The ways in which a business delivers its value proposition to its customers.

4. **Customer Relationships:** The types of relationships a business establishes and maintains with its customers.

5. **Revenue Streams:** The sources of revenue for a business.

6. **Key Resources:** The critical resources that a business needs to operate.

7. **Key Activities:** The most important activities that a business performs to deliver its value proposition.

8. **Key Partners:** The external partners that a business relies on to operate.

9. **Cost Structure:** The costs associated with running a business.

Building Block	Key Questions
Customer Segments	Who are the target customers? What needs do we solve?
Value Proposition	What core value do we provide to customers? What bundles of products/services meet needs?
Channels	How do we reach customers to deliver value propositions? Direct or indirect channels?
Customer Relationships	How do we interact with customers through their lifecycle? What relationships work best?
Revenue Streams	How does our value proposition generate revenue? Transaction fees, subscriptions, etc?
Key Activities	What activities are critical to deliver our value proposition?
Key Resources	What resources do our value proposition and channels require? Physical, intellectual, human?
Key Partnerships	What partnerships are needed to optimize operations? Suppliers, distribution, technology?
Cost Structure	What are the key costs inherent in our model? Fixed or variable costs?

Table: Applying the BMC

The BMC can be used as a tool to analyze, design, and develop a business model. It allows entrepreneurs and managers to identify and address key components of their business model, to better understand their customers and to create innovative and sustainable strategies.

The benefits of using the BMC include:

1. **Improved focus on key components of a business model:** The BMC helps to organize and focus thinking around the key components of a business model and their interrelationships.

2. **Increased collaboration:** The BMC is a visual tool that can be used collaboratively with stakeholders to generate discussion and new ideas.

3. **Simplified communication:** The BMC provides a simple, visual representation of a business model that can be easily communicated to stakeholders.

4. **Enhanced understanding of customer needs:** The BMC encourages businesses to identify and focus on their customer segments and value propositions, which can lead to a deeper understanding of customer needs and preferences.

Overall, the BMC is a useful tool for businesses of all sizes and industries to better understand and develop their business models. Steve Blank, a Silicon Valley entrepreneur and educator is known for using the Business Model Canvas (BMC) in his Lean Startup workshops as a tool to help startups develop and refine their business models. Blank is a proponent of the Lean Startup methodology, which emphasizes rapid experimentation, customer feedback, and iterative development to build successful startups.

Blank uses the BMC as a visual tool to help startups understand the key components of their business model and identify areas for improvement.

During his workshops, Blank guides startups through the process of filling out the nine key components of the BMC: customer segments, value proposition, channels, customer relationships, revenue streams, key resources, key activities, key partnerships, and cost structure.

Once the startups have filled out the BMC, Blank encourages them to test their assumptions by getting out of the building and talking to customers. This customer feedback is used to refine and iterate on the business model, with the ultimate goal of creating a product or service that meets a real customer need and is financially sustainable.

The benefits of using the BMC in this way include increased clarity and alignment around the key components of the business model, a better understanding of the customer and their needs, and a more iterative and data-driven approach to developing and refining the business model. By using the BMC in combination with the Lean Startup methodology, startups are able to reduce the risk of failure and increase their chances of success.

Lean Startup Methodology

The Lean Startup methodology is a business approach that emphasizes the importance of creating a minimum viable product (MVP) and then quickly testing and iterating on it based on customer feedback. The idea is to minimize the amount of time, money, and effort spent on building a product that customers might not want, and instead focus on creating a product that solves a real problem or meets a real need.

The Lean Startup methodology was popularized by Eric Ries in his 2011 book "The Lean Startup: How Today's Entrepreneurs Use Continuous

Innovation to Create Radically Successful Businesses." The key components of the methodology include:

1. **Validated Learning:** The idea of learning quickly and inexpensively through experiments and feedback from real customers.

2. **Minimum Viable Product (MVP):** The smallest version of a product that can be created and tested to validate its potential.

3. **Continuous Innovation:** A process of constantly refining and iterating on a product based on feedback from customers.

4. **Agile Development:** An iterative and flexible approach to product development that emphasizes speed, flexibility, and responsiveness.

Element	Description
Core Features	The absolute bare minimum features that enable the core value proposition
Limited Scope	Focuses on a subset of features, user segments, platforms etc.
Fast Development	Can be built quickly and iterate rapidly based on feedback
Basic UI/UX	Very simple interface and user experience to convey the value
Measurable Metrics	Tracks key metrics to determine if value is achieved
Early Adopters	Targeted to early adopters willing to accept limitations
Gather Feedback	Provides means to gather user feedback for future development
Vision Statement	Conveys the future vision to set expectations on limitations

Table: Elements of the Minimal Viable Product

The Lean Startup methodology can be used by any business, but it is particularly well-suited for startups and small businesses that are looking to quickly validate their ideas and bring products to market. It can be used to test and validate new products, business models, or marketing strategies. By focusing on validated learning, startups can avoid the costly mistakes that often come with traditional business planning and execution.

The benefits of using the Lean Startup methodology include reduced risk, faster time to market, and greater customer satisfaction. By iterating on a minimum viable product and continuously innovating based on customer feedback, startups can create products that better meet the needs of their customers and are more likely to succeed in the market. Additionally, the focus on validated learning can help startups avoid wasting time and money on products or strategies that do not work.

Design Thinking

Design thinking, a problem-solving methodology rooted in a human-centered approach to innovation and design, has become increasingly popular in recent years. It is a versatile methodology that can be applied in various contexts, such as product design, service design, and organizational design. The key principles of design thinking include empathy, iteration, prototyping, and a bias towards action. These principles are often attributed to the work of the design firm IDEO and its founder, David Kelley.

1. Empathy is a crucial aspect of design thinking, as it allows designers and innovators to understand the needs and

experiences of end-users and stakeholders. This understanding is achieved through various research methods, such as direct observation, interviews, and surveys. By putting themselves in the shoes of the end-users, designers can gain insights that help them create more effective solutions.

2. Iteration is another vital element of design thinking. It is a process of continually refining and improving prototypes and ideas based on feedback from end-users and stakeholders. This approach ensures that solutions evolve and adapt to the needs of the target audience, resulting in more successful and impactful outcomes.

3. Prototyping plays an essential role in the design thinking process. It involves creating tangible representations of ideas and solutions to test and refine them. Prototypes allow designers to experiment with different concepts, identify potential issues, and gather valuable feedback to improve their solutions iteratively.

4. A bias towards action is an inherent characteristic of design thinking. It encourages risk-taking, experimentation, and learning from failure in pursuit of innovation. This mindset promotes a culture of continuous improvement, fostering creativity and collaboration within teams and firms.

Design thinking offers various benefits to teams and organizations, such as:

1. A deeper understanding of end-users and stakeholders, which helps create more tailored and effective solutions.

2. A more creative and collaborative work environment that encourages innovation.

3. A faster and more efficient innovation process, as teams can quickly identify and address issues through iteration and prototyping.

4. More successful and impactful solutions, as design thinking focuses on addressing the real needs and desires of end-users and stakeholders.

When applied properly, design thinking is a powerful problem-solving methodology that emphasizes a human-centered approach to innovation and design. By focusing on empathy, iteration, prototyping, and a bias towards action, design thinking can help teams and firms develop a deeper understanding of end-users and stakeholders, fostering a creative and collaborative environment and resulting in more successful and impactful solutions.

Scenario Planning

Scenario planning is a strategic management tool that involves anticipating potential future events and developing multiple plausible scenarios that consider various outcomes. It is a way of thinking about the future and preparing for it, even when there is a high degree of uncertainty or complexity involved. It usually involves a rigorous process of identifying key uncertainties and drivers of change, developing multiple scenarios based on different combinations of these factors, and analyzing the implications of each scenario for the organization's strategy, operations, and environment.

Scenario planning is particularly useful in making strategic decisions pertaining to technology, where the pace of change and uncertainty can be high. By developing scenarios that consider potential technological developments and their impact on the organization, leaders can make more informed decisions about investment, resource allocation, and innovation. The process can also help managers and leaders identify emerging technologies that may disrupt their industry or provide new opportunities for growth. It can also help leaders manage risks and uncertainties associated with technological change. By considering a range of possible outcomes, leaders can better prepare for unexpected events and identify potential risks or threats that may arise from technological developments. Furthermore, scenario planning can help leaders build organizational resilience to technological change. By developing scenarios that consider the impact of technological developments on the organization's strategy, operations, and environment, leaders can better prepare for change and develop strategies to adapt and thrive in a rapidly evolving technological landscape.

Some specific benefits of scenario planning as it relates to technological forecasting include:

1. It enables organizations to consider a range of possible outcomes and prepare for potential disruptions while identifying emerging opportunities.

2. It helps organizations identify emerging technologies and their potential impact on the organization's strategy, operations, and environment.

3. It enables organizations to anticipate changes in customer behavior and preferences and develop strategies to meet their evolving needs.

4. It can help organizations identify potential regulatory changes and ensure compliance with new regulations, and

5. It assists organizations in anticipating changes in the competitive landscape, maintaining a competitive advantage by developing strategies to respond to potential technological developments.

The pros and cons of scenario planning are shown below:

Pros	Cons
Prepares for multiple plausible futures	Substantial time and resources required
Challenges conventional thinking	Outcomes depend heavily on input assumptions
Identifies risks and opportunities	Difficult to gain buy-in and adoption
Provides strategic foresight	Complex process with many variables
Tests decisions across scenarios	Can oversimplify complex realities
Promotes agility and resilience	Scenarios may not cover all possibilities
Enables contingency planning	Perceived as speculative by some
Fosters communication and consensus	Outdated scenarios lose relevance

Table: Pros and Cons of Scenario Planning

DevOps

DevOps is a methodology that combines software development (Dev) and IT operations (Ops) to achieve faster and more reliable software delivery. It aims to bridge the gap between the development and operation teams and promote a collaborative and integrated approach throughout the software development lifecycle.

The foundational concepts of DevOps were initially introduced by Patrick Debois and Andrew Shafer in 2008 at the Agile Conference in Toronto. The concept was further developed and popularized by Gene Kim, Jez Humble, and others. The key principles of DevOps include continuous integration, continuous delivery, and continuous deployment, which involve automating software development and deployment process, ensuring that changes are tested and validated before being released into production, and using feedback loops to continually improve the software. DevOps also emphasizes the importance of monitoring and logging in production environments, which allows teams to quickly detect and resolve issues, as well as gather insights for further improvements. By adopting DevOps practices, organizations can gain a competitive advantage in today's fast-paced digital landscape.

DevOps helps teams and firms to achieve faster and more reliable software delivery, improve collaboration between development and operation teams, reduce the time to market for new products and services, and enhance customer satisfaction. It also helps to promote a culture of innovation, experimentation, and continuous improvement within organizations.

Growth Hacking

Growth hacking is a marketing strategy focused on rapidly experimenting with various tactics and channels to identify the most effective ways to grow a business. Growth hacking was popularized in 2010 by Sean Ellis, who was a startup advisor and marketer, and has since become a popular concept in the world of startups. There are some similarities to the ideas used in lean startups, except the focus is explicitly on aggressive growth.

Ellis identified three foundational concepts of growth hacking: a focus on rapid experimentation, a data-driven approach, and a focus on growth metrics. These concepts are aimed at finding low-cost and scalable ways to acquire and retain customers, and have been adopted by many successful startups. Teams and firms can use growth hacking to quickly test and iterate on new ideas and tactics, allowing them to quickly identify what works and what doesn't. By using a data-driven approach and focusing on growth metrics, teams and firms can ensure that their efforts are focused on activities that are driving real business results. Additionally, growth hacking can be used to help startups and small businesses compete with larger, more established companies by finding innovative and cost-effective ways to grow their customer base. By focusing on data-driven experimentation and creative problem-solving, teams can find new and innovative ways to drive growth and stay ahead of the competition.

Jobs to Be Done Theory (JBDT)

The Jobs to be Done (JTBD) theory is a framework used to understand the motivations behind why consumers "hire" a product or service to complete a specific job or task. The foundational concepts of JTBD were first introduced by Clayton Christensen in his book "The Innovator's

Dilemma". The theory suggests that consumers don't buy products, but rather hire them to perform a specific job in their lives.

According to the JTBD theory, understanding the job that a consumer is trying to accomplish is crucial to creating successful products and services. It focuses on the context of the job, the emotional and social aspects of the job, and the desired outcome of the job. By understanding these elements, teams and firms can create solutions that better meet the needs of their customers. Using JTBD theory can help teams and firms identify new opportunities for innovation, as well as refine existing products and services. It can also help in creating more effective marketing strategies and messaging that resonates with the needs and motivations of their target audience. By its very design, JTBD theory helps businesses maintain a more customer-centric approach to product development and marketing. Over the long run, this approach can lead to increased customer satisfaction and loyalty, as well as improved business performance.

What is clear from the discussion above is that there are a plethora of frameworks and tools available to improve and fine-tune the broad spectrum of solutions that we try to develop in technology strategy. Let us now consider an example of an organization that uses several of these frameworks in order to achieve its goals.

Case Example: Y Combinator

A classic case in point is Y Combinator, a well-known startup accelerator and venture capital firm in Silicon Valley that uses several of these analytical frameworks to jump-start entrepreneurial initiatives, some of which are already familiar to us. These include:

1. **Startup School:** Y Combinator's online platform offers a curriculum for aspiring entrepreneurs, which includes video lectures, articles, and resources on various topics like fundraising, product development, marketing, and growth.

2. **Lean Startup:** Based on Eric Ries' book, this framework emphasizes the importance of validating assumptions and testing ideas through experimentation and iteration. It involves building a minimum viable product (MVP), getting customer feedback, and pivoting if necessary.

3. **Business Model Canvas:** Developed by Alexander Osterwalder, this framework provides a visual tool for mapping out a company's business model. It consists of nine building blocks, including customer segments, value proposition, revenue streams, and cost structure.

4. **AARRR Metrics:** This framework focuses on five key metrics for measuring a startup's growth: Acquisition, Activation, Retention, Referral, and Revenue. It helps companies understand which areas they need to improve in order to achieve sustainable growth.

5. **Pirate Metrics:** Similar to AARRR Metrics, Pirate Metrics is another framework for tracking a startup's growth. It was created by Dave McClure, a venture capitalist and startup advisor. It is based on the idea that startups need to focus on specific metrics at each stage to optimize their growth and achieve sustainable success. It includes five stages: Awareness,

Acquisition, Activation, Revenue, and Retention. The framework emphasizes the importance of user acquisition and retention for long-term success.

6. **OKRs:** Objectives and Key Results (OKRs) is a framework for setting and tracking goals in a company. It involves defining specific, measurable objectives and identifying key results that will indicate progress towards those objectives. This framework helps teams stay focused on what's important and align their efforts towards common goals. OKRs are typically set on a quarterly basis and can be used at all levels of an organization, from individual contributors to executive leadership. By regularly reviewing progress towards OKRs, teams can adjust their strategies and tactics to ensure they are on track to achieve their goals. OKRs are known to increase transparency and accountability within teams.

In addition, Y Combinator provides a number of resources to startups that help them obtain seed funding, refine their ideas, learn from experts, and eventually scale their platform. Some of these are summarized in the table below.

Approach	Description
Seed funding	Provides startups with financial resources to focus on product development and initial traction
Intensive mentorship	Offers guidance from experienced entrepreneurs, investors, and experts to refine business strategies
Weekly dinners	Facilitates peer learning, networking, and collaboration among participating startups
Focus on product-market fit	Encourages startups to adapt to customer feedback and create successful products
Structured deadlines	Creates a sense of urgency to achieve milestones and make rapid progress
Extensive network	Provides access to resources, partnerships, and investment opportunities through a vast network
Post-program support	Continues to support startups with resources, advice, and network access after the program ends

Table: Y-Combinator Resources and Activities

Nowadays, these frameworks are widely used, not just by incubators and accelerators, but also by a wide swath of other organizations to provide structure and guidance to early-stage startups as well as established ventures. By adopting some of the practices and frameworks mentioned above, any firm can encourage and support intrapreneurial activities, and thus create a dynamic and innovation-oriented culture within the organization.

One must recognize that many of the concepts and issues that are being addressed through these frameworks are the fundamental problems that we are trying to solve in the exciting field of technology strategy. As the field of technology strategy continues to evolve, new concepts, frameworks and tools will emerge to make it more relevant to the contemporary landscape.

In Conclusion

The significance of technology strategy in today's ever changing business landscape cannot be over-emphasized. The continual pace of innovation fueled by developments in several cutting edge areas of technology necessitates that enterprises maintain agility and foresight in their strategic planning. Companies have the unique opportunity to harness the power of emerging technologies to build sustainable competitive advantages and drive long-term success. But in order to do that, they need to put technology strategy at the forefront of their decision-making.

We have looked at the fundamental concepts, analytical frameworks, and practical tools and methods that drive technology strategy formulation and implementation throughout this book. We have considered some of the problems and opportunities that technological innovation presents, as well as the crucial role of technology strategy in navigating this complicated landscape. We have sought to give readers a concise grasp of strategic technology management and its impact on organizational performance, productivity, and profitability. In order to do this, we have also drawn on insights from a wide range of complementary disciplines.

Looking ahead, it is obvious that technology strategy will continue to play a growing role in influencing the trajectories of enterprises and entire industries. Technology strategy will continue to be a critical predictor of success in an era defined by rapid innovation and change, from addressing global concerns such as climate change and cybersecurity to driving the creation of new and innovative technologies and business models. We believe that the knowledge base and ideas covered in this book will be a go-to resource for professionals, academics, and students alike, offering the tools and inspiration needed to engage in meaningful and impactful technology strategy engagement. We can ensure that our companies and institutions are not only prepared for the problems of today, but also well-positioned to influence and thrive in the increasingly linked and dynamic world of tomorrow by embracing the premise and the possibilities of technology strategy.

CHAPTER XV

Further Reading

Ansoff, H. I. (1991). Critique of Henry Mintzberg's 'The design school: Reconsidering the basic premises of strategic management'. Strategic Management Journal, 12(S2), 449-461.

Beck, K., et al (2001). Manifesto for Agile Software Development. Retrieved from https://agilemanifesto.org/

Bower, J. L., & Christensen, C. M. (1995). Disruptive Technologies: Catching the Wave. Harvard Business Review, 73(1), 43-53.

Briggs, J., & Kodnani, D. (2023). The potentially large effects of artificial intelligence on economic growth. Goldman Sachs Global Economics, U.S. Economics, January 2023.

Brown, T. (2008). Design thinking. Harvard Business Review, 86(6), 84-92.

Bryson, J. M. (2018). Strategic planning for public and nonprofit organizations: A guide to strengthening and sustaining organizational achievement. John Wiley & Sons.

Camp, R. C. (1995). Benchmarking: The search for industry best practices that lead to superior performance. ASQC Quality Press.

Chakravarthy, B. S., & Doz, Y. L. (1992). Strategy process research: Focusing on corporate self-renewal. Strategic Management Journal, 13(S2), 5-14.

Chesbrough, H. W. (2007). Business model innovation: it's not just about technology anymore. Academy of Management Executive, 18(2), 13-22.

Chesbrough, H. (2003). Open innovation: The new imperative for creating and profiting from technology. Harvard Business Press.

Chesbrough, H. W. (2006). Open innovation: A new paradigm for understanding industrial innovation. In H. Chesbrough, W. Vanhaverbeke, & J. West (Eds.), Open innovation: Researching a new paradigm (pp. 1-12). Oxford University Press.

Christensen, C. M. (1997). The Innovator's Dilemma: When New Technologies Cause Great Firms to Fail. Harvard Business Review Press.

Christensen, C. M., Raynor, M. E., & McDonald, R. (2015). What Is Disruptive Innovation? Harvard Business Review, 93(12), 44-53.

Christensen, C. M., & Raynor, M. E. (2003). The Innovator's Solution: Creating and Sustaining Successful Growth. Harvard Business Review Press.

Christensen, C. M., & Overdorf, M. (2000). Meeting the Challenge of Disruptive Change. Harvard Business Review, 78(2), 66-76.

Clark, K. B., & Wheelwright, S. C. (1993). Managing new product and process development: Text and cases. Simon and Schuster.

Collis, D. J., & Rukstad, M. G. (2008). Can you say what your strategy is? Harvard Business Review.

Cooper, R. G. (1990). Stage-Gate Systems: A New Tool for Managing New Products. Business Horizons, 33(3), 44-54.

Cooper, R. G., & Edgett, S. J. (2010). Developing a product innovation and technology strategy for your business. Research-Technology Management, 53(3), 33-40.

Cooper, R. G. (2019). Winning at new products: Creating value through innovation. Basic Books.

Danneels, E. (2004). Disruptive technology reconsidered: A critique and research agenda. Academy of Management Review, 29(4), 670-686.

Downes, L., & Nunes, P. (2013). Big Bang Disruption: Strategy in the Age of Devastating Innovation. Portfolio/Penguin.

Eisenhardt, K. M., & Sull, D. N. (2001). Strategy as Simple Rules. Harvard Business Review, 79(1), 106-116.

Eisenmann, T., Parker, G., & Van Alstyne, M. (2011). Platform envelopment. Strategic Management Journal, 32(12), 1270-1285.

Conner, B. P., Manogharan, G. P., Martof, A. N., Rodomsky, L. M., Rodomsky, C. M., Jordan, D. C., & Limperos, J. W. (2014). Making sense of 3-D printing: Creating a map of additive manufacturing products and services. Additive Manufacturing, 1, 64-76.

Corbett, C. J., & Van Wassenhove, L. N. (1993). The trade-off between lead time and productivity in manufacturing. Management science, 39(10), 1319-1338.

Damanpour, F. (1991). Organizational innovation: A meta-analysis of effects of determinants and moderators. Academy of Management Journal, 34(3), 555-590.

David, P. A. (1985). Clio and the economics of QWERTY. The American Economic Review, 75(2), 332-337.

Flynn, B. B., & Flynn, E. J. (1999). Synergy in the implementation of quality management and supply chain management. Management Science, 45(5), 659-671.

Gans, J. S., & Stern, S. (2003). The product market and the market for "ideas": commercialization strategies for technology entrepreneurs. Research policy, 32(2), 333-350.

Garcia, R., & Calantone, R. (2002). A critical look at technological innovation typology and innovativeness terminology: a literature review. Journal of Product Innovation Management, 19(2), 110-132.

Garud, R., & Karnøe, P. (2001). Bricolage versus breakthrough: distributed and embedded agency in technology entrepreneurship. Research Policy, 30(2), 277-291.

Gawer, A., & Cusumano, M. A. (2014). Industry platforms and ecosystem innovation. Journal of Product Innovation Management, 31(3), 417-433.

Gibson, I., Rosen, D. W., & Stucker, B. (2010). Additive Manufacturing Technologies: Rapid Prototyping to Direct Digital Manufacturing. Springer.

Hambrick, D. C., & Fredrickson, J. W. (2001). Are you sure you have a Strategy? Academy of Management Executive, 15(4), 48-59.

Hamel, G., & Prahalad, C. K. (1994). Competing for the future. Harvard Business Review Press.

Hamel, G., & Prahalad, C. K. (1989). Strategic intent. Harvard Business Review, 67(3), 63-76.

Hamel, G., & Prahalad, C. K. (1994). Competing for the future. Harvard Business Review Press.

Hamel, G. (2000). Leading the Revolution: How to Thrive in Turbulent Times by Making Innovation a Way of Life. Harvard Business Review Press.

Henderson, R., & Clark, K. (1990). Architectural Innovation: The Reconfiguration of Existing Product Technologies and the Failure of Established Firms. Administrative Science Quarterly, 35(1), 9-30.

Holmquist, S. (2016). 3D Printing in the Automotive Industry: A Case Study. Chalmers University of Technology, Master's Thesis.

Hopkinson, N., & Dickens, P. (2006). Rapid Manufacturing: An Industrial Revolution for the Digital Age. John Wiley & Sons.

Hull, C. W. (1986). Apparatus for production of three-dimensional objects by stereolithography. U.S. Patent No. 4,575,330.

Kahn, K. B. (2018). New product forecasting: An applied approach. Routledge.

Kaplan, R. S., & Norton, D. P. (2008). The execution premium: Linking strategy to operations for competitive advantage. Harvard Business Press.

Kelley, T., & Kelley, D. (2013). Creative confidence: Unleashing the creative potential within us all. Crown Business.

Kim, W. C., & Mauborgne, R. (2005). Blue ocean strategy: How to create uncontested market space and make the competition irrelevant. Harvard Business Press.

Kim, W. C., & Mauborgne, R. (1999). Strategy, Value Innovation, and the Knowledge Economy. Sloan Management Review, 40(3), 41-54.

Kogut, B., & Zander, U. (1993). Knowledge of the firm, combinative capabilities, and the replication of technology. Organization Science, 3(3), 383-397.

Kotter, J. P. (1996). Leading change: Why transformation efforts fail. Harvard Business Review, 73(2), 59-67.

Kouprie, M., & Visser, F. S. (2009). A framework for empathy in design: stepping into and out of the user's life. Journal of Engineering Design, 20(5), 437-448.

Lange, T., Mahoney, J. T., & Pyne, D. (2019). Platforms, systems competition, and innovation: Reassessing the foundations of antitrust policy. Journal of Economic Perspectives, 33(3), 23-42.

Laudon, K. C., & Traver, C. G. (2013). E-commerce: Business, Technology, Society. Prentice Hall.

Leenders, M. A., & Waarts, E. (2013). Collaborative new product development teams and team innovativeness: A review and future directions. Journal of Product Innovation Management, 30(1), 110-126.

Liedtka, J., & Ogilvie, T. (2011). Designing for Growth: A Design Thinking Tool Kit for Managers. Columbia Business School Publishing.

Liker, J. K. (2004). The Toyota Way: 14 Management Principles from the World's Greatest Manufacturer. McGraw-Hill.

Lucas, H. C., & Goh, J. M. (2009). Disruptive Technology: How Kodak Missed the Digital Photography Revolution. The Journal of Strategic Information Systems, 18(1), 46-55.

Malerba, F., & Orsenigo, L. (1993). Technological regimes and firm behavior. Industrial and Corporate Change, 2(1), 45-71.

Markides, C. C. (1997). Strategic Innovation. Sloan Management Review, 38(3), 9-23.

Markides, C. (2006). Disruptive Innovation: In Need of Better Theory. Journal of Product Innovation Management, 23(1), 19-25.

McGrath, R. G. (2013). The End of Competitive Advantage: How to Keep Your Strategy Moving as Fast as Your Business. Harvard Business Review Press.

Meyer, M., & Lehnerd, A. (1997). The power of product platforms. Building Value and Cost Leadership. Free Press.

Mintzberg, H., Ahlstrand, B., & Lampel, J. (2009). Strategy safari: The complete guide through the wilds of strategic management. FT Press.

Murmann, J. P. (2003). Knowledge and competitive advantage in the pharmaceutical industry. Annu. Rev. Sociol., 29(1), 163-185.

Murphy, S. V., & Atala, A. (2014). 3D bioprinting of tissues and organs. Nature Biotechnology, 32(8), 773-785.

Nohria, N., & Eccles, R. G. (1992). Face-to-face: Making network organizations work. Sloan Management Review, 33(4), 83-94.

O'Reilly, C. A., & Tushman, M. L. (2008). Ambidexterity as a Dynamic Capability: Resolving the Innovator's Dilemma. Research in Organizational Behavior, 28, 185-206.

Osterwalder, A. (2004). The Business Model Ontology—A Proposition in a Design Science Approach. Ph.D. Thesis, Université de Lausanne, Lausanne, Switzerland.

Pappas, C. (1984). Strategic Management of Technology. Journal of Product Innovation Management, p. 30-35.

Phaal, R., Farrukh, C., & Probert, D. (2004). Technology roadmapping—a planning framework for evolution and revolution. Technological Forecasting and Social Change, 71(1-2), 5-26.

Porter, M. E. (1980). Competitive strategy: Techniques for analyzing industries and competitors. Free Press.

Porter, M. E. (1996). What is strategy? Harvard Business Review, 74(6), 61-78.

Porter, M. E. (2008). The five competitive forces that shape strategy. Harvard Business Review, 86(1), 78-93.

Ries, E. (2011). The Lean Startup: How Today's Entrepreneurs Use Continuous Innovation to Create Radically Successful Businesses. Crown Business.

Rogers, E. M. (2003). Diffusion of Innovations (5th ed.). Free Press.

Schrage, M. (2000). Serious Play: How the World's Best Companies Simulate to Innovate. Harvard Business Press.

Sims, P. (2011). Little Bets: How Breakthrough Ideas Emerge from Small Discoveries. Free Press.

Stanford HAI. (2023, April 1). 2023 State of AI in 14 Charts. Retrieved from https://hai.stanford.edu/news/2023-state-ai-14-charts

Stanford HAI. (2023). AI Index Report 2023. Retrieved from https://aiindex.stanford.edu/wp-content/uploads/2023/04/HAI_AI-Index-Report_2023.pdf

Sull, D. N., & Eisenhardt, K. M. (2011). Simple rules for a complex world. Harvard business review, 89(9), 68-76.

Sutherland, J., & Schwaber, K. (1995). SCRUM Development Process. In Agile software development with SCRUM (pp. 117-134). Prentice Hall.

Sutherland, J., & Schwaber, K. (2011). The Scrum Guide. Scrum.Org.URL: https://www.scrum.org/resources/scrum-guide, last accessed February 1, 2023.

Teece, D. J. (2010). Business models, business strategy and innovation. Long Range Planning, 43(2-3), 172-194.

Tushman, M. L., & Anderson, P. (1986). Technological discontinuities and organizational environments. Administrative Science Quarterly, 31(3), 439-465.

Tushman, M. L., & O'Reilly, C. A. (1996). Ambidextrous organizations: Managing evolutionary and revolutionary change. California Management Review, 38(4), 8-30.

Ulwick, A. W. (2016). What customers want: Using outcome-driven innovation to create breakthrough products and services. McGraw-Hill Education.

Utterback, J. M., & Abernathy, W. J. (1975). A dynamic model of process and product innovation. Omega, 3(6), 639-656.

Van der Meer, H. (2017). Strategy diamond: The framework for successful growth. Routledge.

Ventola, C. L. (2014). Medical Applications for 3D Printing: Current and Projected Uses. Pharmacy and Therapeutics, 39(10), 704-711.

von Hippel, E. (1986). Lead users: A source of novel product concepts. Management Science, 32(7), 791-805.

Wernerfelt, B. (1984). A resource-based view of the firm. Strategic Management Journal, 5(2), 171-180.

West, J., & Gallagher, S. (2006). Challenges of open innovation: The paradox of firm investment in open-source software. R&D Management, 36(3), 319-331.

West, J., & Bogers, M. (2014). Leveraging external sources of innovation: A review of research on open innovation. Journal of Product Innovation Management, 31(4), 814-831.

Yu, D., & Hang, C. C. (2010). A Reflective Review of Disruptive Innovation Theory. International Journal of Management Reviews, 12(4), 435-452. Zaltman, G., & Duncan, R. (1977). Strategies for planned change. John Wiley & Sons.

Zook, C. (2004). Finding your next core business. Harvard Business Review, 82(4), 66-75.

Check out these other titles by Bharat Rao

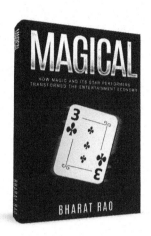

 MINDZEN MEDIA

Made in the USA
Coppell, TX
06 March 2024

29798158R00125